THE ART OF ALMOST ACHIEVING

JD Palmer

*If it's been an adventure
it's been a success!*

My thanks go to my wife
for her ideas and patience

Cartoons: Stephen (hilly) Hill
www.issuu.com/hillymoto

Cover photograph:
A rainbow off the coast of Jersey

Contents

Plenty of time for reminiscing

From the moment we are born, for we humans, life is a series of challenges. Many of them we can't avoid, but some we choose to take on in spite of the risks involved. Fortunately, we are blessed with amazing inner reserves, and when we tap into them, we often surprise ourselves by achieving things that we thought were far beyond us.

Completing the eighty six mile Ridgeway Challenge non-stop on foot is an extreme test, demanding not only physical fitness, but above all mental resilience. The event, which is held every August, is one of the highlights of my year. The route follows the ancient Ridgeway Path from Ivinghoe Beacon in Buckinghamshire to Avebury Stone Circle in Wiltshire. It involves around six thousand feet of ascent as it passes through the counties of Hertfordshire, Buckinghamshire, Berkshire, Oxfordshire and Wiltshire. So far, in five attempts at this gruelling event, I have only managed to complete the full distance twice. The rather modest average speed I manage to sustain over such a distance means that I have to tackle around thirty miles of the route at night by torchlight as I cross the North Wessex Downs. However, for me, this only adds to the thrill and appeal of the event.

Unlike some runners, who appear to me to be nothing short of superhuman, I confess I spend a large part of the time walking rather than running. My approach is to jog down the hills whenever possible, and take it steady when climbing up them. The rest of the time I just do my best to maintain a brisk walking pace. I may be wrong, but in endurance events, it always feels to me as if there are far more uphill sections than downhill sections! It is easy to allow the prospect of tackling such a long distance to overwhelm you. I dispel my fears and misgivings by following the example set by my boss where I used to work. Every January, faced with the challenge of achieving a seemingly impossible Sales Target for the coming year, he always started his pitch to his staff by saying, "Remember, how do you eat an elephant?" and we would all chant in unison, "One bite at a time!"

The most common question my family and friends ask me is, "Tell me, why do you do it?" I usually fob them off by saying that it gives me a target to aim for and forces me to keep fit all year in readiness, but that is not why I do it. My real reason is simply that it is an adventure, and in spite of my advancing years, adventures are still just as important to me as ever. I enjoy being out on mountains and hills, away from life's daily routines, and I like to test myself by attempting to do things that I am not sure I can.

The next question people ask is, "Out there alone, with nobody to talk to, what on earth do you think about for all that time? You must get so bored!" In fact, nothing could be further from the truth. I find plenty to think about, and it is the many, some may say bizarre thoughts that occupy my mind during my long 'pilgrimage' to Avebury that are the subject of this book. In a light-hearted manner, I have recalled my thoughts and feelings throughout the many hours it took me to complete the Ridgeway Challenge in 2021, one month before my seventy fifth birthday.

As mile after mile rolled by, as well as taking in the beautiful changing landscapes around me and making frequent checks on my progress, a constant stream of random thoughts kept popping into my head. I had flashbacks to many half-forgotten episodes that had occurred during my life when I had taken on some sort of personal challenge. Some of the challenges were quite minor things, while others required a major sustained effort on my part, but every one of them stretched me and moved me out of my comfort zone. As I plodded on, I chuckled to myself as I recalled one of the more humorous things that had happened.

When the event was over, I spent some time trying to rate my performance objectively on each of the challenges I had been thinking about, comparing my actual performance with what I had optimistically expected of myself beforehand. I gave myself a mark out of ten for each of them, and the results of the exercise are shown in the candid self-assessment chapter later in the book.

I find that walking through the countryside on my own has a relaxing, calming influence on me, at times almost a spiritual one. I only have myself to worry about, and my mind is freed from distractions and everyday responsibilities, allowing it to freewheel and think with more clarity about life. As it takes me around twenty seven hours to complete the eighty six miles to Avebury, I certainly have plenty of time to think and reminisce. During that time I experience a full gambit of feelings and emotions ranging from determination to doubt, from hope to despair, and from fatigue to elation. For me it is always a rollercoaster ride, but what an adventure, what a fantastic way to spend a weekend! For me, it is the very stuff that life is made of.

The Ridgeway Challenge (86 miles non-stop)

The Ridgeway Challenge is organised and run by the Trail Running Association. Almost all of the route is on footpaths and bridleways, with just a few sections on minor roads. Farm machinery uses some of the tracks, and recreational vehicles are allowed to use some of the western sections during part of the year. In places they make deep ruts which are often overgrown by grass and sometimes filled with rainwater. These can be very treacherous for those hurrying along on foot, especially at night.

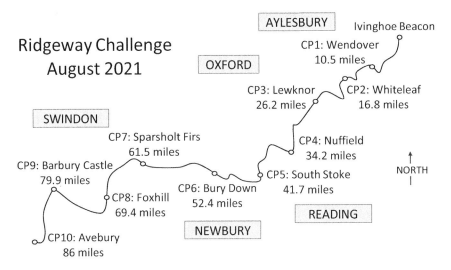

The Ridgeway Path's history stretches back over 5000 years. During that time it has been used by drovers and travellers, and may even have been used by the legions of Rome. Starting from Ivinghoe Beacon, the first half of the route takes you through the rolling countryside of the picturesque wooded Chiltern Hills. The path then descends into the Thames Valley and runs along beside the River Thames for a while, eventually crossing it at Goring. The second half of the route takes you over the more isolated North Wessex Downs, high up on breezy chalk ridges, passing close to several old hill forts and ancient settlements. Finally, the path descends past fields littered with Sarsen stones to arrive in the village of Avebury. It is a walk through history.

The organisation of the event is excellent, and runners are well cared for at each of the ten checkpoints by volunteers, often from local running clubs. Water and a variety of snacks are available at each checkpoint, and coffee and hot food are available from the half-way point onwards. Entrants for a 10 o'clock start are counted as a 'finisher' if they complete the distance in under twenty eight hours, while the faster runners who enter for a 12 o'clock start are only allowed twenty six hours.

As I am now a 'senior citizen', I can do with as much time as possible, so I enter for the 10 o'clock start. If I entered for the 12 o'clock start I would risk not making the first few checkpoints before their cut off times. It is a sobering thought that by the time I arrive at the halfway checkpoint by the Thames, the fastest runners who started some two hours after me are around 40 miles ahead of me nearing Avebury!

Whatever level of runner you happen to be, ranging from an elite runner through to someone more like me, as with all endurance events, completing them depends on many factors. However well you have physically prepared yourself, without the right mind set your performance will suffer. The weather also plays a major part in your performance, as I have found out to my cost on two of my Ridgeway Challenge attempts when it was particularly hot. If it happens to be wet, then as well as it being unpleasant, you are almost certain to get blistered feet. An element of luck is also involved. For no obvious reason, I definitely run better on some days than others, and there is always the possibility of picking up an injury by tripping up or treading awkwardly on the uneven terrain.

From my point of view, there are three 'phases' to the event:

1. Before the event, physically preparing myself in the months leading up to it, and then on the day getting to the start line on time, mentally prepared, and fully hydrated.
2. Completing the event itself in under twenty eight hours.
3. After the event, rehearsing and embellishing tales of my daring exploits so that I can bore people over the next few months if they are foolish enough to ask me how I got on.

The following chapters describe my progress through each of the ten checkpoints along the route. As well as describing the route itself, I relate some of the random and often rambling thoughts that pop into my head. As fatigue and a lack of sleep take hold of me, my state of mind fluctuates from being clear and lucid to being what I can only describe as slightly deranged.

1 : Ivinghoe to Wendover (10.5 miles)

At last I am at the start line of the 2021 Ridgeway Challenge after months of preparation. I have registered and had a tracker taped to my rucksack so that my progress, or lack of it, will be displayed on the Ridgeway Challenge website for the world to see. I feel in good shape, and excited at the prospect of the adventure ahead. My rather anxious wife kisses me goodbye. She constantly worries that I am past it and is sure I will end up lying 'somewhere out there', twitching in a ditch and being pecked by birds, only to be dug up years later by Time Team. I actually get away at 10:04, and she takes a hurried snap as I fly past. As usual, in her haste to take it she centres the camera on another runner. I find out later that I do appear in the photograph, but in the extreme righthand corner with my trailing leg cut off. She has been taking similar photographs of me in action ever since I first met her over fifty years ago. Back at home we have a selection of them in the album where we have been on holiday or I have run in marathons and other events. When old friends visit us, after a few drinks we often play a game where we get the albums out and they have to try to spot me in the photos.

As always, I set off in high spirits, optimistically hoping that I will do well and not let myself down. This year we are starting in batches of about ten runners at Steps Hill because of Covid 19 restrictions, which is a short distance from Ivinghoe Beacon. Once through the trees a panoramic view opens up. From high on the hill, I can see for miles to my right. Ahead I can see Bledlow Ridge standing out in the distance. It is about twenty miles away if you follow the snaking Ridgeway Path, but more like fifteen miles as the crow flies.

For no particular reason, my mind wanders back to my early school days. I remember the first proper 'decision' I ever made. When I was nine years old, I was in the school Christmas play. I was a 'Page' holding the cloak of one of the Three Kings. At the rehearsal, we were all belting out 'We Three Kings' for all we were worth, when Miss Kelly the music teacher suddenly stopped us and said, "Who's singing flat?" She made us each sing individually until the culprit was unmasked. It was me of course, although I thought my singing sounded pretty good. To add insult to injury, she then told me to mime when we performed. At that instant, I remember deciding that however long I lived, I would never again sing in public. In all honesty, I don't think my refusal to sing has been much of a loss to the world of music.

At school, I used to enjoy cross-country running events. Strangely though, everybody else in my class seemed to hate them and tried to dodge them. I always did well in them, and usually finished in the top few runners. However, looking back now I can see that my 'success' was really somewhat inflated and rather hollow, because in my innocence, I hadn't realised that it was considered cool by my classmates to bait the games tutor by purposely not trying to do one's best. The poor tutors had a lot to put up with. However, they never seemed to relate to us as individuals. Everything was geared to keeping us in order and managing us. Any show of spirit was quickly suppressed by them. We were taught by rote in all subjects, and I never remember ever being asked for my opinion about anything. I hope things are rather more liberal at school these days.

I jog down the steep chalky path of Steps Hill and on up Pitstone Hill. The view to my right is tremendous. The track descends into thick woodland, and after winding through the wood for some time I descend to a road. Watching out for cars, I turn right and jog down the pavement past Tring railway station. I am moving at quite a steady pace, but already runners are continually passing me. I feel a strong urge to quickly get some miles behind me, but I have to resist the impulse. I keep reminding myself that it is vital that I run my own race at my own comfortable pace, and don't allow myself to be influenced when other runners pass me.

Back in the first year of my secondary school, I had to do metalwork as a subject. Our tutor was Mr Beggar (we didn't call him that) who had been in the army. In his loud booming voice he told us to stop what we were doing and all stand around the drilling machine. Fifteen of us, all in our freshly pressed aprons our mothers had made us, stood in a semicircle around the machine. "I'm going to tell you the names of its parts, but listen carefully because I will only tell you once." He had a habit of pointing with a stick and banging it down on things, which made us all very jumpy. He pointed out various parts of the drill, flicking the stick about in a menacing manner. "Headstock. Drilling table. Chuck." He reeled off about ten names, as all fifteen of us frantically repeated them under our breath over and over again as he moved on to the next one. "What's this?" he said looking straight at me. "The H-H-H-Headstock sir," I said. He ignored me, and his gaze wandered onto the boy standing to my right. I relaxed. As he progressed through the parts, the boys who had yet to be asked got visibly more and more stressed. Everyone was praying that when their turn came he would point to a part they could remember. Although intimidating us in that manner was brutal, I must admit that it worked, because I can still remember the names of the parts over sixty years later. On the other hand, in all that time, nobody has ever asked me to reel off the names of the parts of a drilling machine!

The first time I remember feeling I had really achieved something significant was when I learnt to swim at the age of thirteen. Most of my friends had been swimming for years, but in the 1950s there were polio scares linked to public swimming pools, so my parents had not allowed me to go. I have my games tutor to thank for taking the trouble to help me with the basics and get me started.

I jog and walk intermittently along a long narrow track until I reach a slender concrete footbridge spanning the A41. The adrenalin rush at the start has subsided and I feel calmer now. I cross the bridge and set off across a large field which has plenty of evidence of cows underfoot, although no cows are in sight. I walk beside a tall hedge which curves to the left, hiding the far gate where I will exit the field. I am hoping that when I reach the end of the hedge I don't find a herd of cows blocking my way. I don't mind encountering the odd cow now and again, but I am wary of tangling with a whole bunch of them.

Some years ago I was out running on footpaths through the fields where I live. I went through a gate which had a printed note stuck to it which I couldn't read because I didn't have my glasses on. I ran across the field weaving my way between several grazing cows. There were also some calves, and gradually the whole herd started to run around getting more and more agitated. Ahead of me on the path was an extra-large cow just standing glaring at me. Too late I realised it was a bull! I turned to retrace my steps and there on the path some distance away, blocking my retreat, was a second bull. I am told there is never more than one bull in a field, but on that day I swear to you there most definitely was! I veered off the path and accelerated down the hill towards a distant hedge. I have never run so fast in my life. Eventually, I arrived at the far gate, heart pounding. Since then, I always give livestock of any sort a very wide berth.

I stay on the well-marked track crossing a few minor roads and along a tree lined avenue with extensive views to the right as the ground falls steeply away. I arrive at the village of Hasthoe, which seems to be one long road with old cottages and houses on the left. I'm not hungry because I had a good breakfast, and also topped up just before I set off. However, to keep my energy up I must eat regularly so I have an 'Energy Gel' and a banana. I can never squeeze a gel out without getting it all over my fingers.

I went on my first trip to the mountains of North Wales in 1961 on a Duke of Edinburgh Award expedition. It was also the first time I had ever camped. We were all driven the two hundred odd miles in an old Bedford van with vague and wobbly steering that the school had hired. We arrived in the Ogwen valley just as it was starting to get dark. It was the first time we had ever seen the tents, and we had a difficult time working out how to erect them.

We happy breed, we band of brothers …..

Fortunately, the tents were 'state of the art' for the time in that they had sewn in groundsheets. My friend and I lay in our tent, coughing and spluttering as we puffed away at untipped French cigarettes. Daring and grownup as this seemed to us, it did nothing to stop us feeling the penetrating cold, as we were lying directly on the groundsheet with nothing to insulate us. The first morning, I unzipped the door flap, and snow that had fallen overnight fell into the tent. Peering out of the flap, snow-covered Tryfan towering above us looked completely unclimbable.

I was one of a team of four lads who planned to walk twenty miles in two days over the mountains to gain their Bronze Award. On the morning of the third day of camping at our Ogwen base camp, I set off with my team on the two day expedition. We were already cold, grumpy, tired and hungry before we set off, which did nothing for team spirit. We struggled north with our heavy backpacks, and finally reached the ridge halfway between Carnedd Daffyd and Carnedd Llewelyn. As we gained the ridge, we were almost blown off our feet by the strong wind rushing up from Anglesey. We had not been prepared for the violence of the wind, because we had not realised that we had been walking up on the ridge's sheltered side. Eventually, we worked our way along the ridge safely all the way to Foel Fras, and down to Aber where we set up camp for the night.

By the end of the second day's walking, we were out of rations and all famished, and to make matters worse we were also out of cigarettes. One of the team, who went by the nickname 'Aerial' (I can't think why), found a battered packet of dates at the bottom of his rucksack, and I turned up a tin of condensed milk in mine. Our little 'band of brothers' sat there by Llyn Cowlydd like a bunch of shipwrecked mariners, eating dates and taking turns to sip condensed milk from the tin. How good it tasted!

My feet were in a shocking state because I was wearing new boots which I had only worn once before. They proved to be the worst form of torture ever invented. The following year when I did my Silver Award I hired some boots at a shop in Capel Curig. Experience is a wonderful thing!

I carry on jogging through Hasthoe while I can, but have to start walking again at the end of the village as the road starts going uphill. At the top of the hill I go through a gate into Pavis Wood. I pass a farm on my right and then descend steeply down a rocky gully in the woods. The rocks make jogging difficult, and

I almost miss a Ridgeway sign taking me sharp left out of the gully. I must concentrate more! I walk through more woodland, and then as the path starts dropping, I jog downhill on a long rough path which widens out into an unmade road for vehicles.

As a child, I loved playing football in my street, which was a long 'close'. In the 1950s there were hardly any cars to worry about. If a car did come up the road we would all stop playing and get out of its way. We would line up on the pavement and salute it as it went by.

The day came when the games tutor at school was going to select my year's school football team. On the day of the selection, which would be my one and only chance to get in the team, I was off school ill. The following week, while the selected team practised on the field in full kit, the geography tutor took the rest of us for a kickaround in one of the playgrounds. In our game, I felt I played like a hero in a class of my own, and scored three great goals. After a while, the games tutor called by to ask how we were all getting on. To my dismay I overheard the geography tutor say to him, "The score's four nil. One lad scored three goals, but I think it was more by luck than judgement." Normally, I don't bear grudges, but I never forgave him the whole time I was at school, and I dropped geography as soon as I could.

The powers-that-be decided that to improve the image of the school, we would henceforth stop playing 'footer' and only play 'rugger'. I hated rugby, and was not built for the game, physically or mentally. One disastrous year the so-called Asian Flu epidemic struck the UK. There were so many pupils off sick, that in desperation, even I was picked for the rugby team. The next game was against a local school who liked to think themselves a cut above the other schools in the area. They took the game very seriously. I remember feeling intimidated when they arrived with their coach and started stretching and limbering up as they put on their head guards. Our team stood there quaking, looking to our Welsh woodwork tutor, who managed the team, for encouragement and support. However, his pep talk merely turned my deep depression into absolute despair.

The horror show that unfolded was probably the worst couple of hours of my young life. I was put in the middle of the scrum as 'hooker' and only remember an interminable series of bruising encounters. Time after time I would be the last man to pick myself up from the mud after the scrum had collapsed on me, dazed and disoriented, only to hear the whistle being blown for the next scrum a few yards away. I am not particularly religious, but I remember praying for the final whistle to blow to bring the nightmare to an end. Suddenly it was over. We had lost, but I didn't care. I was just grateful that I had survived with a few minor bruises.

I jog past several large dwellings, and catch sight of the Wendover checkpoint about half a mile ahead. The checkpoint has been set up by the roadside on the eastern outskirts of Wendover. I feel I have made a good start, and looking at my GPS watch I see that my average speed so far is encouraging. I calculate that if only I can keep up this average I will do it in twenty hours! Who am I kidding? Of course I won't be able to keep it up. It would be great to do it in under twenty four hours though. Oh well, only around seventy five miles to go!

Wendover checkpoint

Arrival time at checkpoint: Saturday 12:32

Stage distance: 10.5 miles
Time taken to complete the stage: 2:28
Average speed for the stage: 4.25 mph

Distance since starting: 10.5 miles
Time taken since starting: 2:28
Average speed since starting: 4.25 mph

Distance left to Avebury: 75.5 miles

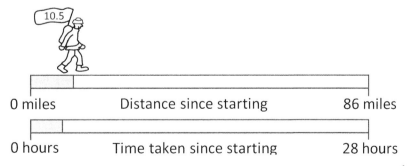

0 miles   Distance since starting   86 miles

0 hours   Time taken since starting   28 hours

2 : Wendover to Whiteleaf (6.3 miles)

After topping up my water supplies I am off again. I walk past a lovely church and then alongside a clear stream until I reach the high street where I turn left. I walk through the town and over a bridge that spans both a railway and a major road. The pavement is on the right side of the road, and around half a mile up the hill the road bends sharply to the right. I have to take care crossing the road close to the blind bend. I follow the Ridgeway sign through a gate into the trees.

At primary school I remember always wanting to be the leader of the gang. When I was aged about ten, at school I wrote, directed and starred in a play about my hero King Arthur. In fact, I remember being torn between playing the part of King Arthur and the part of Sir Lancelot. At that age, Queen Guinevere seemed a bit superfluous to the plot, and to be honest, a bit soppy anyway, so I wrote her out. Any psychiatrist reading this book will note that even at an early age I was exhibiting clear signs of an Orson Welles complex.

Subsequently, on many occasions in life I've tried to take the lead, only to look around and find nobody was following me. At work I would enthusiastically float an idea, only to instantly lose my audience when a colleague, presumably with more charisma than me said, "Does anybody fancy going down the pub?" In fact, my enthusiasm and passion for a topic often seems to turn people off! Some people just seem to have a natural talent for leadership, but I suspect anyone's leadership skills can be improved by a good mentor. I have noticed that in a group of people, different situations demand different leadership qualities, and I have been surprised how often the right leader emerges in response to a challenge that presents itself. Personally, I've always had respect for leaders who show that they are competent. I don't look for perfection in a leader, and I am willing to forgive any minor shortcomings I find. I am more suspicious about those who project an air of confidence without doing anything much to justify it. However, over the years I've always had problems with 'authority figures'.

I chuckled to myself as I remembered something the actor Peter Ustinov said on the subject. A housemaster at a public school, which had a reputation for turning out our future politicians and captains of industry, wrote an end of year report to Lord Benson, the father of one of his pupils. The report concluded: "Barnaby has made some progress this year, but he is not a born leader, yet."

I follow a chalk path that first leads me up a series of steps past a quarry, and then continues steeply up Coombe Hill. This is tiring work if you try to hurry. The path leads to a large memorial which commemorates the fallen of the Boer War. From the monument there is a fantastic view in nearly all directions. My legs are doing fine, but I can tell that even after only twelve miles, they have already lost some of their spring. I have no time to stop and admire the view so I bear left and jog down the long grassy hill.

Throughout my teenage years, I was keenly interested in the Space Programme. I envied the Russian and American astronauts as they took their first daring steps into space.

Imagine the state of my cockpit after a 5G turn!

There was no prospect at that time of a UK astronaut going into space, so I saw my destiny as being a Lightning pilot in the RAF. Inspired at school by John Gillespie Magee's poem 'High Flight', I dreamt of 'slipping the surly bonds of earth, and dancing the skies on laughter-silvered wings' as he had.

It was probably for the best that I discarded that particular dream somewhere along the way. I had conveniently

17

overlooked the fact that as a passenger in a car I was a poor traveller. I frequently felt car sick because of its motion, especially when looking at a map or book. Can you imagine the state of the cockpit if I was piloting a Lightning and trying to read the instruments while pulling a 5G turn?

In later years, I did try a one week gliding course at Lasham Aerodrome with a friend. It was quite an experience. I sat in the front seat of a two-seater machine with a laconic Australian instructor sitting behind me. He claimed he could tell how tense his pupil was by studying the hairs on the back of their neck. We were towed to a height of around 2000 feet by a light plane, at which point we released the tow by pulling hard on a lever, twice. It was an exhilarating experience, almost silent except for the rushing sound of wind when you were diving. Move the stick to the right and you roll right as your right wing drops, but you also yaw to the left which you have to correct with some right rudder. Practising the stall was the most dramatic thing. Pull back on the stick and the speed drops off as the nose goes up. At a certain speed one of the wings stalls, and suddenly the controls go mushy. Push the stick forward to gain flying speed again and regain control, then pull back slowly to get out of the dive. You lose a lot of height in the manoeuvre, so it's best not to do it on purpose when you are too low.

On my third flight, the instructor told me to take control for the tow. As we started trundling across the grass, all of the hairs on my head, as well as those on my neck were bolt upright. Compared to the tow plane, a glider has a very low wing loading, and consequently gets airborne almost straight away, whereas the tow plane struggles to get off the ground. It is very easy to rise far above the tow plane and lose sight of it under your nose. The tow line is then pulling the rear of the tow plane upwards, which makes it even harder to get the tow plane off the ground. By my fifth take-off I was able to make a reasonable job of it. I don't know what they pay those tow plane pilots, but whatever it is, it's not enough!

I also tried a two day introductory course on paragliding in the Peak District. I enjoyed it, and given time I think I could become quite good at it. We spent the first day learning how to 'inflate' a large fabric wing behind us as we stood at the top of a steep grassy slope. We then shouted 'Geronimo' and charged down the slope straining against the pull of the wing. In spite of our instructor extolling us to put more aggression and effort into our runs so that we got airborne, disappointingly none of us managed to.

On the second day, our instructor revealed the cruel trick he had been playing on us. He produced a much larger wing, which must have had twice the area of the one we had been charging down the hill with all of the previous day. He explained that the smaller wing would never support our weight, but was great for getting students to really fling themselves downhill. I was first to have a go with the larger wing, and I was immediately airborne. It was a fantastic feeling. As a novice, there was no chance of soaring around as you see experts do with their tapered wing paragliders. All I did was to weave my way farther down the hill as the ground kept dropping away beneath me. I had many such flights that day, but was probably never more than fifty feet from the ground. Sometimes I managed to flare at the last moment and land on my feet, and other times I just landed in an ungainly heap. What a great weekend that was!

I am now winding my way through quite a dense wood, still descending, being careful not to fall over the tree roots. There is no single path now, just several options all heading in the right general direction. I arrive at a gate and cross a field that takes me into the Chequers Estate. This is the Prime Minister's country house, built sometime in the 16th century. I can see the house clearly across the fields, and there are M.O.D. warning signs, but no fences! I wonder how many C.C.T.V. cameras I am on?.

In my early twenties, my friend Dave, who was a keen car enthusiast, had a tuned up wide wheeled Renault. From time to time he entered amateur rallies held on local country roads. On one occasion, his regular navigator was not available, and he asked me to take on the role. Like a fool, I said I would. I've always liked making things, and I decided that what a rally navigator needed was a proper map board with some illumination for the map because the event was being held after dark. I constructed a plywood map board with a little pedestal for a lamp which could be plugged into the cigar lighter socket in the car. With the wisdom of hindsight I know I should have tested it out before the event.

I met Dave outside the social club in the factory grounds, and as we walked up to his car, I detected a faint smell of petrol where he had just topped up. It made me feel a bit queasy, and I immediately regretted having the hamburger and pint of lager while I was waiting for him. The first problem reared its head as soon as I sat in the car. My map board was far too big. I had to move my seat much farther back than was comfortable to fit the board on my lap. In fact, I was so far back that I didn't have much of a view through the windscreen. The second problem quite literally came to light when I plugged the lamp into the cigar lighter. The lamp was unguarded and much too bright. It was impossible to see anything outside the car. All we could see when we looked at the windscreen was two wizened faces staring back at us. I tied a handkerchief around the lamp, which at least gave him a sporting chance of seeing the road, and also gave me a sporting chance of seeing the map.

Dave never asked me to navigate again!

Things went downhill from there. The competitors were being sent off one minute apart, and as we moved up to the start line, he revved the engine in readiness. Our turn came, and a rally official thrust the course instructions to me through my open window, banged twice on the roof, and Dave lifted the clutch. To the sound of screeching tyres I was pinned back in my seat, as if by some giant hand, and the route instructions slid off the board somewhere onto the floor. Within seconds, while I was still fumbling around the floor, inhibited by my oversize map board, we arrived at the factory gates. "Left or right?" he yelled. I was still trying to work out which way when the next car arrived beside us and turned right. "Right!" I said, and we were off. Not for long however, as I soon needed to stop because I was feeling so unwell. When we did get going again, all I remember is that our rally came to an abrupt end when I directed him down a narrow lane which took us to a farm gate displaying a warning sign saying 'No entry, Foot and Mouth disease'.

The rally was won by one of Dave's friends in a bog standard Austin A30 whose girlfriend was navigating. Apparently, because it was on public roads, the rally was designed so that high speed wasn't required, just sound map reading skills. He never asked me to navigate for him again.

I am leaving Chequers now, going up a long hill into some woods. The track is now bending around to the left skirting Pulpit Hill. It's time for more food, so I eat a jam sandwich and treat myself to a couple of flapjacks. I descend again and cross a road with no pavement. Turning left, after a few yards I come to the Plough pub which is in the village of Cadsdene. I ignore the many families sitting relaxing in the gardens in the sunshine, drinking and eating. More runners are still streaming past me.

I always seem to drink too much water in the early stages of an event. Consequently I have to nip discreetly off the path into the bushes from time to time. On this occasion, as I stood there stationary, wasting precious seconds, the thought occurred to me, "What if my tracking device isn't working and I have some sort of turn and keel over right here and now? How long would it be before I was found?"

I would probably be missing for ages unless somebody else nipped into the very same bush as me, and what are the odds of that happening? Even if somebody did nip into the same bush as me, what are the odds of them having a defibrillator with them?

I once estimated the cumulative time I waste in the bushes on this event to be somewhere in excess of fifteen minutes! One year, I speculated on whether, during the hours of darkness when I could be sure nobody was near me for miles, I could save valuable time by 'going' while I was still walking. I realised this would be no mean feat and wondered if adopting some sort of crab-like sideways gait for 50 yards or so was a possibility. I didn't actually experiment with the technique though because it was such a windy night!

Just past the pub I turn right and go through a gate. I slog slowly up Whiteleaf Hill for about a quarter of a mile which is the steepest section on the whole eighty six mile route. I manage to climb it without pausing, but only just. Another runner catches me up and asks me how much longer the hill goes on for! At last I am at the top of Whiteleaf Hill, and I'm relieved the stiff climb is behind me. It really took it out of me. I'm becoming aware of the continual mental pressure I'm having to put myself under to keep pressing on. It's so tempting to ease up on the pace, and if you don't concentrate, your pace can gradually drop back to your natural walking speed without you realising it. I carry on through the woods for some distance and then see the Whiteleaf checkpoint ahead. I top up my water and grab a banana.

Whiteleaf checkpoint

Arrival time at checkpoint:	Saturday 14:13
Stage distance:	6.3 miles
Time taken to complete the stage:	1:41
Average speed for the stage:	3.75 mph
Distance since starting:	16.8 miles
Time taken since starting:	4:09
Average speed since starting:	4.05 mph
Distance left to Avebury:	69.2 miles

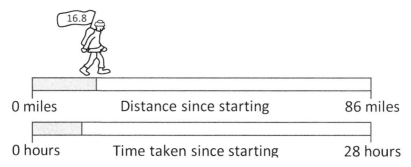

0 miles   Distance since starting   86 miles

0 hours   Time taken since starting   28 hours

3 : Whiteleaf to Lewknor (9.4 miles)

I leave the checkpoint, thanking everyone for their support, and after a few hundred yards I come to a lane. I turn right onto it and after thirty yards turn left onto a track. The track divides into two. Should I go straight on or branch left here? This is one of the few places on the whole route that could do with a sign. Actually, I don't think it matters which track you take, as long as you stay in the field and keep going downhill. I go straight on and come to a gate at the far end of the field. I turn right following a faint path in the grass, staying in the field. I arrive at a gate, beyond which are a long flight of steps. I try to go down them at speed, but the steps are an awkward distance apart, so I slow down and take them one at a time. The path becomes a rough road which I go down for about a mile passing several houses. I reach the A4010 which is quite a busy road. I haven't seen many cars since I left Wendover. A right turn would take me a short distance into Princes Risborough, but I turn left and walk along the pavement. Several runners go flying past me as I hurry off up the road.

When I was sixteen, much to my parents concern, I became the proud owner of an ancient smoky Villiers two-stroke motorbike which I rode to school every day. I must have looked a rare sight because my leather jacket was two sizes too large, and my crash helmet was one size too small. My dramatic and noisy arrival at school in the mornings, engulfed in a blue haze, caused much amusement among my classmates. I seemed to be the only one who realised just how cool I really was.

When I passed my driving test the following year, I upgraded my motorbike to a 1951 Ford Popular 1172cc side valve car which I bought from my uncle for twenty pounds. It was unkindly christened by some, the 'sit-up-and-beg Ford Pop'. It had tiny feeble headlamps, no wing mirrors, no seatbelts, no heater, no radio, no central locking, no washers, no electric windows, no heated rear window, no flashing direction indicators, cable operated drum brakes, no hydraulics or brake servo, manual steering, no water pump, no catalytic converter, extremely narrow tyres, and only three gears with no synchromesh on first gear. It could only manage a top speed of around 45 mph flat out at which speed your senses were assaulted from all sides by rattles and ominous clonking noises. However, it did have a starting handle and a couple of dozen grease points that needed attention every three thousand miles.

In spite of its primitive design, I look back fondly on the experience. I yearn for the simplicity of a car where you can open the bonnet and recognise each component, and not be confronted by anonymous black boxes as you are these days. It was a car you could easily service and repair yourself. However, rather stupidly I took the cylinder head off to carry out a completely unnecessary decoke and warped the head. From then on, the cylinder head gasket blew on a number of occasions when I went up a long steep hill. Mostly though, I look back with tremendous nostalgia at the adventures I had in it. I can remember to this day the intoxicating smell of leather and hot engine oil. I loved driving it. Maybe though, all I am really remembering is being young. It's a sobering thought that there are now twice as many people living on our planet as there were then, and many more than twice as many cars driving about.

I walk away from Princes Risborough at a brisk pace for about a third of a mile, going slightly uphill. At a junction I cross the road and turn right onto a minor road. I go straight on at crossroads and left into a field following a Ridgeway sign. I continue on across a large field of wheat passing several people, who it turns out are not part of the event. At the far end of the field is a metal gate, and just through the gate are two Race Stewards who greet me. They are guiding each runner safely across a railway line by keeping a lookout for approaching trains. By this stage in the event, fatigue can easily impair a runner's judgement.

When I was in my forties, while I was on holiday in North Wales with my family, I noticed a poster which had been left in place, advertising the annual Snowdonia Marathon which had taken place the previous week. At that time, I never dreamt that I would ever be capable of running such an extreme distance. However, it caught my imagination, and I decided to have a go the following year. When I got home I bought my first pair of running shoes. I trained throughout the coming year, gradually building up the distance I could run. Eventually I could manage a fifteen mile run once a week. To my delight, and surprise, I managed to complete the marathon in 4 hours 45 minutes the following year.

24

Since then, I have completed the Snowdonia Marathon a further twenty times. The strange thing is that my times now are still around the five hour mark, which is only a bit slower than they were thirty years ago!

The Snowdonia Marathon has a well-deserved reputation as a tough marathon. The first four miles take you up the Llanberis Pass during which time you gain over eight hundred feet of height. Over the next eight miles you descend around one thousand feet to reach the village of Beddgelert at around the half marathon distance. This means that in spite of the long slow climb at the start, the long downhill section means that you can still set a good time for the first half of the marathon. I have frequently fooled myself by looking at my watch at Beddgelert and thinking, "Wow, I'm on fire today!" However, experience has taught me that you expend a lot more effort completing the second half of the marathon than you do completing the first.

As you leave Beddgelert, the road starts to climb, and you notice the effects of gravity again. You feel heavy in your legs after the long descent, as gravity pulls against you instead of pulling in your favour. It is an arduous three mile climb out of the village, and I always fight to keep running all the way. Breaking into a walk there is a bad idea. I once made the mistake at Rhyd Ddu of eating a digestive biscuit that a kind soul offered me. I had no saliva, and it was like trying to eat blotting paper. It was several miles before I managed to spit it all out.

The next six miles are reasonably flat until you arrive at the village of Waunfawr. I usually manage to run like a hero the whole way to Waunfawr non-stop, which is a distance of about twenty one miles. At that point, I start to feel confident that I have matters under control.

However, next comes the sting in the tail. The side road out of Waunfawr climbs steeply up the hillside and becomes a muddy track. You quickly gain around seven hundred feet of height, which is very challenging at this stage in a marathon. In spite of trying my best, in all my attempts, I have never managed to run up that hill. I have always had to walk most of the way up it. Near the top, in wet weather, the track becomes an ankle-deep running stream.

At the exposed windy top of the hill, Bwlch-y-groes, the terrain flattens again and the track weaves its way through an old slate quarry past a line of sweet-smelling pine trees. On one occasion I was feeling all in, running along the top in driving rain and strong winds, and feeling really cold and tired, when I ran past a farm Land Rover. A man stood by the open back and shouted to me, "Would you like a hot cup of tea?" I couldn't believe my ears. How had he managed to get up the track with hot tea? He gave me a sugary cup of tea which had an instant and miraculous effect on me. Filled with renewed energy, just a few hundred yards later I was able to look down into the valley at the town of Llanberis. It was only a couple of miles away, and it was now downhill all the way to the finish.

I would never have believed that my state of mind could flip from a feeling of extreme fatigue and almost despair to feeling energetic and optimistic in the space of a couple of minutes! However, the last downhill stretch into Llanberis can be very treacherous, and I have witnessed many runners getting injured there. The steep descent starts on wet slippery grass, and it is easy for a tired runner to take a tumble. I always go slowly and ignore the streams of less cautious runners who go barrelling past me on their way down. Of course, the best part of all is running down Llanberis high street to the finish. The glorious feeling of elation that I experience never wanes, however many times I do the event.

I cross a field, and then a minor road and start ascending Lodge Hill, which is a deceptively steep and sustained climb. It seems to go on and on, and the gradient appears to steepen nearer the top rather than reduce. High up, I go through a hedge onto a wide plateau where a herd of cows are making the most of the lush grass. What a quiet serene place this is, but there is no time to stop. I go back into trees and descend a widening track that provides access to the houses on my right. The track twists and turns, and when I get further down into the valley, it bends left and then straightens. I can see for maybe half a mile ahead. To my right I can hear a steam train chugging along. The Ridgeway Path goes straight on over a road, but if I turned right down the road I would come to Chinnor Railway Station which is where the steam train must be from. Several runners go rushing past me. They are definitely running, not jogging, and are probably elite runners who started two hours after me, who will be among the first to reach Avebury. How do they keep that pace up all day?

As a young man, my old Ford Pop proved to be my passport to freedom. On Saturday nights, once I was going to work, I would go dancing, often to the Trade Union Hall at Watford Junction. In our trendy language we referred to it as 'going up The Trade'. I usually arrived, liberally dowsed in Bay Rum hair tonic which I had been reliably informed would turn me into a babe-magnet, at least for a few hours.

Several live pop groups played there, who later became famous. At half time I remember nipping out to the local pub up the road with my friends for a meat pie and a drink to give us some 'Dutch courage' in the second half. For reasons that escape me now, I thought the sophisticated drink to have was a 'Rum and Black'. Little did I realise at the time that the blackcurrant in the drink left stains at the corners of my mouth, which my mates of course didn't point out to me.

Appearing to have a permanent leering grin on my face which made me look like 'The Joker', could not have done much to improve my chances when we returned to the dance for the second half.

It was very dark in the hall, and it was so crowded that you didn't have enough room to dance properly. You would walk up to a girl and ask if she wanted to dance, and if she did, there was just room to hold her close (after all that was the whole point) and pirouette slowly on the spot. I remember my friend Pete causing a bit of a stir when one dance number finished. As he tried to disengage from the young lady's embrace he found that his chewing gum had somehow got caught up in her long hair as they had danced cheek to cheek. Their frantic efforts to untangle the 'stringy' mess was not a pretty sight, and obviously did nothing for his chances with the girl!

If you felt brave, didn't chew gum, and had had enough Rum and Blacks, you might ask a young lady if you could escort her home. The ace up my sleeve was of course my gleaming Ford Pop waiting down the road ready to whisk her, or more accurately, to trundle her to her home, provided of course that it started, there was enough petrol in the tank and the head gasket held out. If you were lucky enough to be giving a young lady a lift, because it was so dark in the dancehall, you only had a chance to get a really good look at her once you were both outside. By that time you were committed to providing transport, even if you were less attracted to her under the unforgiving glare of the streetlight than you had been in the flattering gloom of the dancehall. More disappointing still were the rare occasions when she turned out to be a real stunner, way out of your league, and you saw the expression on her face when she saw you properly for the first time.

How one's fond memories can deceive one! My memories of the Trade Union Hall with its grand entrance, its flashing lights and its large stage were shattered recently when I happened to walk past it again. It's still there after all these years, but seen in daylight it looks like a slightly upmarket Scout Hut! By the way, if any younger readers are considering applying Bay Rum to their hair, save your money, it definitely doesn't make you a babe-magnet.

I press on along a track that is more or less straight for about four miles, and cross several minor roads. I walk briskly, sometimes breaking into a jog. I decide it's time to eat some more food. One of my wife's little foibles is to put each item of food I take into its own individual bag, and then put those bags into yet another bag. Actually getting at the food in my rucksack while I am on the move is rather like playing 'pass the parcel' at a Christmas party. Eventually I can hear traffic, which can only be coming from a major road. I cross the A40 and continue along the track. On this stretch, I am walking through the National Nature Reserve, and the rough ground to my left slopes up to Beacon Hill. A short time later I pass under a large concrete bridge which carries the M40 motorway. The traffic noise is now loud and continuous. After a quarter of a mile I arrive at the Lewknor checkpoint. I seem to be making good progress and I'm still feeling in reasonably good physical shape.

Lewknor checkpoint

Arrival time at checkpoint: Saturday 16:50

Stage distance: 9.4 miles
Time taken to complete the stage: 2:37
Average speed for the stage: 3.59 mph

Distance since starting: 26.2 miles
Time taken since starting: 6:46
Average speed since starting: 3.87 mph

Distance left to Avebury: 59.8 miles

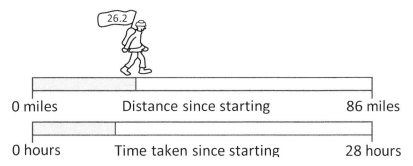

0 miles	Distance since starting 86 miles
0 hours	Time taken since starting 28 hours

4 : Lewknor to Nuffield (8.0 miles)

No time to waste so I top up my water bottle and off I go again. At least I have got a marathon distance behind me. The track carries on in a straight line parallel to a lovely wooded ridge half a mile to my left. After about three miles I cross a road that would take me into the market town of Watlington if I were to turn right onto it. Several runners overtake me. One mystery that I haven't been able to solve is that many of the runners who overtake me say "Well done!" as they pass. Given that they are clearly doing so much better than me because they are overtaking me, often at quite a lick, why are they saying well done to me?

In my sixties after I retired, I had many short breaks on weekdays in North Wales staying bed and breakfast at the Dol Gam guesthouse on the A5 near Capel Curig. Fortified by their wonderful breakfasts, I went for long walks on my own in the surrounding mountains. Two occasions stand out in my memory, which I can remember in detail as if they happened only last week. Real adventures have that effect on you, and are never forgotten.

On one occasion I walked over nearby Moel Siabod, then along its long ridge down to the Pen-y-Gwryd hotel. I then walked up to Pen-y-Pass and around the Snowdon Horseshoe going over Crib Goch, Snowdon and Lliwedd. Somewhat tired, I walked back on the grass verge beside the road to Capel Curig and Dol Gam.

Another time, I walked along tracks past Llyn Geirionydd, over to Llyn Crafnant, and then over to the Llyn Cowlyd dam. I continued over the next ridge to Llyn Eigiau and then climbed up onto the Carnedds arriving on the ridge between Foel Fras and Drum. I stood there admiring the views towards Anglesey, and drank the rest of my now lukewarm coffee. I continued south along the ridge to Carnedd Llewelyn and down the Water Board track to Llyn Ogwen. I then returned along the track beside the A5 to Capel Curig and so back to Dol Gam. The owners of Dol Gam, who are a Welsh-speaking family, provide excellent hospitality. I always feel rather awkward that I don't know how to pronounce the names of their local mountains properly. When they asked me where I had been walking I think they were genuinely impressed with the distance and terrain that I had covered. I must have walked around thirty miles on rough ground, going up and down over several three thousand foot peaks. I certainly slept well that night, and enjoyed my breakfast the next morning.

On long stretches of straight track it is very easy to lose concentration and just keep ploughing straight on. I cross a small road, and about one mile later I spot the Ridgeway sign that directs me left off the main path into a field by a farm. I go up a narrow track in trees at the edge of a large field. It steepens more and more as I start ascending the wooded hill ahead called Swyncombe Downs. I stop briefly to find some more food in my rucksack. I have half a bottle of Lucozade Original and some flapjacks. I try a jam sandwich, but it tastes rather bland. I find myself near the top of the hill in pine trees, and the ground under my feet is soft and springy. The path goes downhill out of the wood into an open field. It dips and then climbs up to a road which I cross. I jog past the 11th century St Botolph's Church on my left as the track bends right. The long wall of Swyncombe House is to my left. Once again, it is easy to miss the next sign. The main path continues straight on, but a sign directs me sharp left, steeply up a green field full of noisy sheep and into a wood.

It was the beautiful long solitary walks that I did in my sixties in the Snowdonia mountains that sparked my interest in attempting the challenging Welsh 3000s route. There are fourteen peaks in North Wales which are over three thousand feet high, spread throughout three mountain groups. To the south is the Snowdon group, to the north of that is the Glyder group, and to the north of that is the Carnedds group. I had walked over all of them several times, but never tried to string them all together in one continuous walk. This results in a challenging walk of over twenty miles from first peak to last peak, during which you notch up over eleven thousand feet of ascent. A secondary challenge is to try to do the walk non-stop in less than twenty four hours.

As often happens with challenges such as this one, somebody with exceptional abilities comes along and sets a blistering record which remains unbroken for many years. In 1988, a fell runner named Colin Donnelly managed to do it in the incredible time of four hours nineteen minutes!

There are various ways to link the fourteen peaks, some starting from the Snowdon group in the south and working their way to Foel Fras, the most northerly peak, and others starting from Foel Fras and working their way south to Snowdon. The difficulty you face when attempting it alone without any support team is getting from your base to the start point, and then getting from the finish back to base. After much thought, I decided to camp in the Ogwen valley and do the route from north to south.

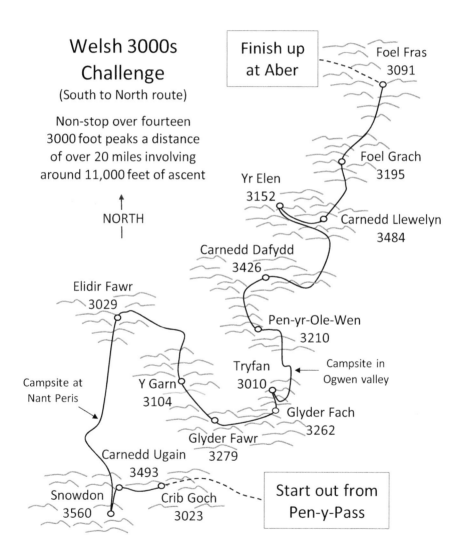

Welsh 3000s Challenge

(South to North route)

Non-stop over fourteen 3000 foot peaks a distance of over 20 miles involving around 11,000 feet of ascent

↑
NORTH
|

Finish up at Aber

Foel Fras 3091

Foel Grach 3195

Yr Elen 3152

Carnedd Llewelyn 3484

Carnedd Dafydd 3426

Elidir Fawr 3029

Pen-yr-Ole-Wen 3210

Tryfan 3010

Campsite in Ogwen valley

Campsite at Nant Peris

Y Garn 3104

Glyder Fach 3262

Glyder Fawr 3279

Carnedd Ugain 3493

Snowdon 3560

Crib Goch 3023

Start out from Pen-y-Pass

I have made five attempts to do the route on my own so far, and have gained much experience of what not to do in the process. On my first attempt, I left Ogwen at 8 o'clock in the evening and walked up to the summit cairn on Carnedd Llewelyn. It was an exhilarating experience to be on my own at night at the top of a mountain. It was a clear night, and in the distance I could see the lights of ships heading for Liverpool. Even though it was August, it was decidedly nippy, so I put on my hat, gloves and all of my spare clothing. I lay down in the cairn just as I was, and made myself as comfortable as possible on the rocky floor.

At about 1 o'clock in the morning I heard the sound of a helicopter approaching. There was a slight breeze, and the top was by then engulfed in cloud. The noise got louder and louder, and I could detect the characteristic sound of a twin rotor Chinook which the army use, and which I have often seen training in the area. I could see nothing through the mist as it hovered some distance above me. The pilot must have been using night vision equipment to have been flying that low in the mountains at night, and I imagine he would be seeing me as a hot thermal image down in the cairn. The last thing I wanted was to cause him to land to rescue me, so I wriggled about a bit to show him I was alive and kicking. After a few minutes the helicopter went away.

At 3 o'clock, by the dim light you get when the dawn sun is still below the horizon, after a yoghurt, I set off north to Foel Fras which would be the starting point of my walk. By the time I reached Foel Fras it was a bright sunny morning.

Back south I went, until I got to Pen yr Ole Wen, where I turned left down the ridge. I carefully descended the only scramble so far, taking extra care because I was on my own. I descended the soggy stretch to the Ogwen valley where I called in at my camp site to pick up some food and water.

The next section was the scramble up the north ridge of Tryfan. This took a lot out of me, and drastically reduced my average speed so far, which up to then had been good. I passed the two rock pillars at the top known as Adam and Eve, and continued south. I descended to the col and then instead of tackling Bristly Ridge, I slogged up the scree to the left of it. On across the Glyders I went, then down the scree and up to the top of Y Garn. I stood there a while assessing my situation. The isolated peak of Elidir Fawr stood ahead of me. I was feeling fine, and still felt I had plenty of energy, but I had taken far too long to get this far. It was around 6 o'clock in the evening, and I would have to tackle the Snowdon group at night with a torch on my own. I felt it would be too risky, and decided to call it a day, and descended down to the campsite in the Ogwen valley. I felt elated that I had done so well on my first attempt. It had been a great experience and I had learnt a lot.

On my next two attempts I followed the same route. On both attempts I left the Ogwen campsite at 3 o'clock in the morning and walked up to the start at Foel Fras over Carnedd Llewelyn by torchlight. I then immediately turned tail and started off south. In both cases the temperature by late morning was at a record level, and I gave up as I fried in the heat. On both occasions I only made it onto the Glyders, and having given up, struggled to make it back down to the camp site, feeling quite groggy on the way down to Ogwen.

He jumped in the air as I rose from my 'grave'.

On my fourth attempt, I went up from the camp site to Foel Fras in the evening. A few hundred yards from the stone marking the summit of Foel Fras I found a suitable trench between the rocks to make myself comfortable for the night,

34

and to keep me out of the wind. I opened my plastic survival bag from its envelope, wriggled into it, and covered myself with a foil blanket. My sleep was disturbed first by a flock of noisy sheep passing by, and then by several wild ponies who were charging about. At about half past three in the morning I was disturbed yet again, and was apprehensive to see the silhouette of a man standing just ten yards away from me. I slowly sat up. As I rose from my 'grave' in my foil blanket, the poor man saw me and jumped in the air from the shock. Once we had both composed ourselves, we had a brief and rather awkward chat. He lived locally, and frequently walked along the ridge to see the sunrise. I remember thinking to myself, who is the craziest, you or me?

An hour later, I could see well enough by the dawn light, so I decided to set off. When I came to fold up my emergency survival bag I found that, due to air trapped in it which I couldn't get rid of, it was much more bulky than it had been when I bought it. I stuffed it into my rucksack as best I could, had a bite to eat, and started walking.

As things turned out, I was not on form that morning and I only got as far as the summit of Tryfan before I felt exhausted and decided to call it a day.

However, on my fifth attempt, I made it all the way to Snowdon, but alas not non-stop, so not 'in style'. I got as far as Pen-y-pass, by around 9 o'clock at night. Again, I did not want to take the risk of going over Crib Goch alone in the dark, so I walked a few hundred yards up the Pyg Track and found a large coffin-shaped rock to lie down on. I covered myself in a foil blanket and used my rucksack as a pillow. It rained. I was then in my late sixties, and I chuckled to myself as I pictured my dear old mum saying, "What on earth do you think you are doing? You'll catch your death of cold!"

Incredibly, I did sleep for some hours. I was awoken around 5 o'clock by a noisy group of walkers going by. I must have looked suspicious lying there, and they gave me a wide berth and went on their way. I ate the last of my supplies which consisted of a banana and a yoghurt, and set off up Crib Goch. Eventually I arrived on Snowdon and spent an hour or so in the café drinking coffee and taking a rest. I felt elated. Fatigue and drowsiness set in as I slowly descended down the Pyg Track to Pen-y-Pass where I caught a bus back to the Ogwen campsite. What an adventure it had been. From Foel Fras to Snowdon had been an elapsed time of around thirty hours, but I had stopped overnight at Pen-y-Pass for about nine of those. I felt really proud of myself. However, as I hadn't managed to do the route non-stop, I already knew I would be back for another attempt one day to do it properly, to do it 'in style'.

The main problem with all of my attempts had been that I expended far too much energy getting to the start point. As I started the route, I was already lacking sleep, and I had used up a lot of energy ascending the Carnedds to get to the start point. In 2021, I decided to have another go with the support of an outdoor adventure company who could provide a guide and transport to get to the start and back from the finish. Their preferred route was from south to north, and it proved to be a much better route than my original choice of north to south. Also, as the attempt was scheduled for June, the days would be at their longest.

We set off from Pen-y-Pass at around 4 o'clock in the morning after a taxi ride up from the camp site in Nant Peris. I was in a group of five people with our Team Leader named Stu, who was a qualified Rock Climbing instructor and First Aid trainer. We climbed Crib Goch and then pressed on to Snowdon at a measured pace. We stood on the summit of Snowdon at dawn as the sun came up, looking down on the clouds. It was a wonderful sight. We walked down beside the railway line until we were opposite Nant Peris, way down below us in the Llanberis Pass. Our steep descent from there was on wet slippery grass, which although downhill, was surprisingly tiring. We were back at the camp site in Nant Peris by around 8 o'clock where we were given a breakfast of bacon rolls and hot coffee. The weather was perfect. It was mild with just a little breeze. I knew I would stand a much better chance with the support of this outfit!

We toiled up the long steep, seemingly endless, track to the summit of Elidir Fawr, then on to Y Garn. Stu kept an eye on all of us and looked after us well. I was still going strongly as we started up the steep scree onto the Glyders.

It was going up the scree that I started to slow noticeably compared to the rest of the group, and I began to feel a bit concerned I was holding the team up, although nobody complained. Once on the Glyders I recovered, and after jumping up and down on the Cantilever taking photographs in the customary manner, we turned north just past Bristly Ridge and descended the scree to the col just short of Tryfan. How much easier it was going down this scree compared to going up it using my north to south route! As our party started to scramble up Tryfan, I fell quite a way behind, and shouted up to Stu that I would stay put while they carried on, and sit it out until they came back down. Looking back at moments of decision such as this, you are always tempted to ask yourself, "Could I have carried on? Did I just take the easy way out? Should I have pushed myself much harder, or was I just being sensible?" However, it's no good regretting previous decisions while sitting in an armchair later in front of the fire. You can never recall the exact conditions or recall exactly how you were feeling. It is better to simply use the experience to help you next time you have to make a decision in similar circumstances.

After half an hour, during which time I rested, the team reappeared. We then descended the rough path on the east side of Tryfan to the camp site where some more food and coffee was waiting for us. I felt fine after a further rest as we sat drinking our coffee. I agonised over whether I should carry on. I think my reasoning at the time was a bit vague and muddled. The members of my group were all supportive, but I would hate to have slowed them down or spoilt their chances of finishing. On the other hand, was I being far too sensitive? If I had carried on, one of them may conceivably have turned out to be slower than me later on. You can never tell in these sorts of endurance situations. If I had carried on and I had slowed them down a bit, would they have actually cared anyway? However, even if I did make it to the end now, I had already 'blown it' by missing out the summit of Tryfan!

I decided to call it a day there, and wished the rest of the group luck as they set off with a fresh Team Leader. How I would have liked to be with them! They all made it safely to Foel Fras, and so achieved the challenge in under twenty four hours. The whole experience made me more determined than ever to successfully complete the challenge. I am looking forward to having another crack at it with the same outdoor adventure company in June 2022, and I have already booked my place. Applying some 'twisted logic' to the situation, maybe it's just as well that I didn't manage to get to the finish in 2021, because if I had, I probably wouldn't be looking forward to attempting it again in 2022.

I toil up the steep wooded path stumbling on tree roots as I go. As I finally exit the wood, the path bends to the right and takes me past a large tractor into the middle of a group of barns. Further on is an impressive mock-Elizabethan house called Ewelme Park. I carry on past the house and through a high hedge. In front of me is a large cornfield, maybe a quarter of a mile across, going downhill. I can see that beyond the far boundary hedge it leads into another field which is not quite so large. This is one of my favourite places on the Ridgeway. I am certainly feeling the distance in my legs now, and I'm much more aware of the constant pressure to keep going without stopping for a break. My mood lifts as I take the opportunity to jog all the way down the field, through the hedge, and on across the next field. After the slog up the hill to Ewelme Park, it feels almost effortless to jog down here. The path disappears into a wood and winds to the left. After a few hundred yards, I come to a gate at the side of the A4130.

A few years ago, my wife happened to read out the programme of the local leisure centre, and mentioned some new classes for senior citizens. Among them were Tap Dancing classes. When I said I would like to have a go at them, you could have knocked her down with a feather! I think she thought I would go once and that would be the end of it. However, I really enjoyed it. I have never been musical, but I get real satisfaction from mastering the different steps, each of which produces a series of clicks of varying tempo and quality. I'll never be a Fred Astaire, but who cares? At home, we have a seven foot by seven foot downstairs cloakroom with parquet flooring where I can practice. To wind up my fellow 'tappers', I refer to it as my 'Dance Studio'. When I'm in there I can't get too carried away though, or I risk colliding with the toilet or wash basin.

During Covid 19 lockdown, when my younger son was upgrading his electronic piano keyboard, I bought his old one and several beginners guides. I started to learn to play it, having never played a note before in my life, and I've made reasonable progress. My party piece is Greensleeves, although my family are all now thoroughly sick of it. I guess they don't appreciate a real 'artiste'. Tap Dancing and the piano have both been good for my mental and physical co-ordination as I transition from being just 'old' to being really 'ancient'. I must say, it's a relief to have got the difficult years for men behind me (i.e. from fifteen to sixty five).

The road is so busy I have to wait for a minute or two to get across. I follow the path which veers to the right away from a roadside pub. The path takes me into Nuffield Golf Course. Rather vague signs direct me across several fairways, until I see the clubhouse ahead of me. I walk just to the right of the clubhouse as yet more runners overtake me. I come to a metal gate, and just the other side is the Nuffield checkpoint near Nuffield Church, reputed to be around nine hundred years old.

Nuffield checkpoint

Arrival time at checkpoint: Saturday 19:10

Stage distance:	8.0 miles
Time taken to complete the stage:	2:20
Average speed for the stage:	3.43 mph
Distance since starting:	34.2 miles
Time taken since starting:	9:06
Average speed since starting:	3.76 mph
Distance left to Avebury:	51.8 miles

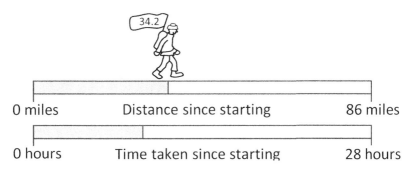

0 miles	Distance since starting	86 miles

0 hours	Time taken since starting	28 hours

5 : Nuffield to South Stoke (7.5 miles)

I grab a banana and top up my water. I put on my jacket, and then carry on. Just thirty yards down the road I turn off left into a field. After a few hundred yards the track turns right along a tree lined gully. This is the start of the famous Grim's Ditch which stretches ahead as far as I can see. I'm feeling a bit low now, but I must press on. In the distance I can just make out a group of horses grazing in a field, which reminds me of my riding exploits.

I had some riding lessons in my early thirties. I remember one of my first lessons when my instructor had my horse on a lunge rein so that I could walk around her in a circle. She warned me that I was about to go into trot, and gave the command "T-rot!" I was completely unprepared for how violent the up and down motion of the trot would be, and for the first time realised the sheer power of the animals. Subsequently, when I had mastered the 'sitting trot' the experience was a bit more comfortable. I progressed, but never really mastered the canter properly. I would always lose my stirrups after just a couple of strides.

However, I could ride well enough on docile horses to go on a hack in a group. When we were on holiday one year I went on a hack in a group with my daughter at a local riding school. I was on a particularly big horse, and they had to bring out a plastic milk crate for me to stand on to mount it. As we walked the horses out of the school following the leader, I distinctly overheard two grooms talking as we passed. One of them pointed anxiously in my direction and said to the other one, "Oh no, you haven't put him on Percy have you?" My horse just plodded along, so as all seemed well I ignored the remark. We had a pleasant walk into the fields and along sunlit tracks. After a while, the leader dropped back to me and said, "We're approaching the cantering spot, and Percy does like to be at the front." I just sat there doing nothing, but Percy took charge and made his move. He plodded past the other riders, with me sitting on him like a sack of potatoes, trying to appear to be in control.

We got to the front of the line, and as we reached a gap in the field boundary hedge, from behind I heard the leader shout, "That's the cantering spot!" I could feel Percy squirming and coming alive under me. His whole body turned slightly away from where it had been pointing, and Percy took off like a bat out of hell. I lost my stirrups which bounced up and down spurring him on to greater and greater things. I clung on for dear life and prayed hard. After about half a mile, the track started to go uphill and without me doing anything, he pulled up to a juddering halt, wheezing away like a steam train. I sat upright, having been slumped over his neck, and twisted in the saddle to look behind me. I could see the others way behind coming my way. I think Percy must have done this on every hack! The other riders congratulated me, and seemed genuinely impressed with the show I had put on for them. It was only the leader who knew that, in fact, I had simply been Percy's latest 'passenger'.

Percy took off like a bat out of hell.

Back home, from time to time I went out on hacks locally. On one occasion, I went to a stable near Knebworth Park to join a group hack. When I arrived they explained that nobody else had booked, but that I was welcome to go out alone. They fixed me up with a sturdy looking horse. As I tried to ride down the lane from the stable they were feeding the other horses, and my horse seemed very reluctant to leave. With great difficulty I managed get out of sight of the stable, down a lane and through an open gate into Knebworth Park. I then spent almost half an hour, with aching legs, coaxing the horse to slowly walk across the park to the far side. As we reached the far fence I turned him slightly to the right intending to follow the perimeter track. On sensing a change of direction, he immediately turned one hundred and eighty degrees and galloped at full pelt back towards the stables. I lost the stirrups as usual and clung on around his neck. At one point I looked up and saw a flock of sheep directly in our path. I now know exactly how Moses must have felt when he parted the waters, because when I thought all was lost, as if by magic, the flock parted in the middle into two groups. They shot off to the left and to the right as we thundered through the gap. Within less than a minute, we were back at the gate in the lane, which was now firmly shut. I made numerous attempts to open the gate, but it's a difficult operation when you are perched on the back of a large grumpy horse. Eventually, I gave up and dismounted to open it. The horse's resentment towards me knew no bounds. Every time I put my foot in the stirrup and tried to mount him, he pivoted away from me. Eventually, worn out, I suffered the final humiliation of leading him back down the lane and into the stable. That was the only part of the whole excursion that the horse seemed to enjoy.

A few years ago, while working with a small group of volunteers mending fences at the local Riding for the Disabled Association stables, the manager came over to us and explained that they were having a problem with novice students. When the students first learnt to mount a horse from the mounting platform, after a few attempts, the horses started to get fidgety and move about. She asked if we could build some sort of 'dummy horse' for them to practise mounting before they encountered the real thing.

Now, I think she had vague ideas of us constructing something along the lines of a barrel with a bit of carpet thrown over it, but my friend Twig and I rose to the challenge. We visualised a wooden horse even the Trojans would have been proud of. It took us several months, but the final result exceeded everybody's expectations. Woody, as we named the horse, is life-sized and can be equipped with a normal saddle and bridle. He has been used to help several new riders to get started and has also proved his worth on the induction course run for new volunteer helpers. Last time I looked in on Woody in the classroom, somebody *had thoughtfully put a rug on him to keep him warm, and pinned a runner-up rosette to his bridle. One of the youngsters had also optimistically stuffed hay in his mouth!*

The light is starting to fade, and once in the trees it gets really gloomy. It is quite uneven underfoot, and there are plenty of tree roots lurking in the gloom ready to trip me up. I decide it's time to turn my torch on before the light fades any further and I fall and injure myself.

I have been married for over fifty years and my wife and I have had very few arguments. We have never argued over money matters, or how to bring up the children. The only thing we fall out over is the setting of the house heating thermostat. I can't stand being in an overheated room, and she can't stand being in a chilly one. I often say to her, "Better not to overheat the house, or when you go out you won't feel the benefit. You'll feel really cold." Her usual reply to this is, "There's absolutely no chance of that! It's warmer out there than it is in here!"

My children all take my wife's side, and claim that they remember the house being like an icebox when they went to bed when they were young. We often had a job to get my youngest son to go to sleep. Just when I thought I had got him settled in bed, he would ask a question to try to keep us talking and prolong matters. His favourite question was, "How did my bones get inside my flesh?" My stock answer was, "Go to sleep now. Ask your mother in the morning."

It's getting darker and darker as I walk along Grim's Ditch, which is a rather spooky place. It is very quiet now and there is nobody else around. It's amazing to think how many centuries people have been walking along this path, which follows an ancient earthwork for over three miles. It was constructed around 800 A.D. and nobody is sure what its purpose was. Sometimes the path runs along inside the gully, and sometimes along the top of the bank beside it. I know I should be eating more, but I don't really fancy anything. Forcing myself, I eat a couple of flapjacks and a banana. I cross two minor roads and eventually arrive at the A4074 which is very busy with fast moving traffic. I cross the road onto the track that enters the trees opposite. After about a third of a mile the track turns left and goes past some houses and

43

several college buildings. I carry on as the track, with hedges both sides, goes through the middle of a golf course.

I like to think I am a balanced, mature and non-judgemental person, although my wife thinks that my politics are slightly to the right of Genghis Khan. When we are watching anything political on TV, I only have to get as far as saying, "If I was in power..." and she quickly leaves the room before I can expound my election manifesto to her.

For the record, my three favourite rants, which would form the backbone of my manifesto, are as follows:

1. *I would stop hospitals charging for car parking which to my mind is just plain wrong.*
2. *I would ban people from singing descant, which completely spoils my personal enjoyment of a good tune. Many of my favourite carols and hymns have been completely ruined when an elite bunch in the choir have chosen to start trilling off piste!*
3. *I would ban well known classical music and cherished pop songs from being used in adverts to sell washing powders, holidays and toilet cleaners.*

There is a slight breeze now, and I begin to feel a bit chilly. As I cross a field, ahead of me I can see the lights in the village of North Stoke. I know that the village looks very pretty in daylight, but I can't see much of it in the gloom. I walk down the short high street past a pub on my left. As I pass the pub which is brightly lit up inside, I can suddenly hear loud voices in animated conversation. Just as quickly, the voices fade as I carry on into the night by torchlight. I am approaching the half way point, and I am surprised how tired I am feeling. After all, when I'm on holiday in Jersey, on one of the days while my wife has a day in St Helier I usually walk right around the island's coastal path with no difficulty.

On holiday, our base is a flat we rent on the coast overlooking St Aubin's Harbour. The coastal path is a beautiful walk, with stunning views across to the French coast and the other islands. I start off walking west, and then turn north along the five mile beach of St Ouen's Bay. The eighteen mile rocky north coast is then a whole series of small bays that you first descend into, and then laboriously climb back out of. It reminds me very much of the coast of Cornwall. I always have a break around the half way point at Mad Mary's Café for a welcome coffee. After reaching the medieval castle at Gorey, the rest of the circuit is walking on roads beside the sea. In all, around half of the distance is on rough paths, while the other half is on coastal roads. I usually complete the circular walk, which is a distance of forty eight miles, in just over fourteen hours. On my return to St Aubin, after a cup of tea and a bite to eat I feel fine.

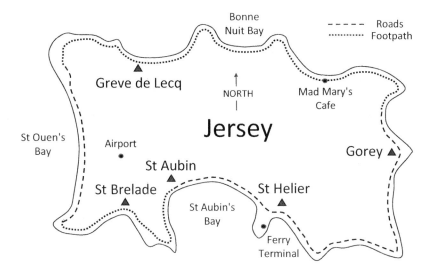

So why is it that I feel so much more tired after walking around forty miles on the Ridgeway than I do after walking forty eight miles around Jersey? After all, as far as physical demands go, there's not that much difference in the two situations. However, in Jersey I don't have any real time constraints and my enjoyment comes from having a relaxed walk in beautiful surroundings. On the Ridgeway Challenge, I am constantly conscious of the time. The surroundings are also beautiful, but my enjoyment comes from completing the full distance within the time allowed. In Jersey I don't want the walk to ever end, whereas during the latter stages of the Ridgeway Challenge, I just want it all to be over!

Near the end of the village I take a right turn which takes me past some lovely cottages, and into a churchyard. I hasten through the churchyard with my torch beam playing on the gravestones. I like to think that I don't get spooked easily, but I must confess that if somebody was waiting there, and suddenly jumped out and said "Boo!" I think I would die of fright. I put any thoughts of being stalked by flesh-eating zombies out of my mind as I hurry on out of the churchyard! The path is now just a vague indentation in the grassy bank running alongside an almost black River Thames. I continue for a couple of miles, with large pleasure boats occasionally going past upriver holding parties onboard with music blaring and loud voices. Then just as suddenly, silence and darkness again. The experience is surreal, and has a feeling of other-worldliness about it. I am starting to get quite cold now.

Unexpectedly, I won an award at work which meant that as an engineer, I could join a group of sales colleagues on a trip to the Goodwood Racing Circuit where we would have the chance to drive a variety of cars around the circuit. Some of my sales colleagues owned fast cars themselves, such as Porsches and BMWs, and were immediately able to hare around the circuit like Stirling Moss. I was used to driving a Morris Marina 1.3, and found the circuit somewhat more challenging than they did. I just felt lost out there on such vast expanses of tarmac. At speed it was so difficult to tell how fast to approach a corner, and in some cases, which way the corner turned and how tight it was. There were so few visual cues to help you. Each driver was only allowed a limited number of laps, so it was not possible in the time available to significantly improve your driving technique.

We were first taken around the circuit by an instructor in a Ford Sierra. We then swapped seats in the pits and it was my turn to drive. As I accelerated out of the pit lane, I did nothing for my credibility by remarking that the acceleration was rather disappointing considering that the car had a 2.8 litre engine. The instructor remained inscrutable and quietly pointed out that the acceleration would have been much better if I had started off in first gear rather than in third!

The fastest car they let us loose in was a clapped-out Formula Ford single seater. Before it was our turn we each had a series of photographs taken of us from different angles as we sat posing in the car complete with crash helmet and racing overalls, trying to look like Steve McQueen. Once our 'photoshoot' was over we had a turn at driving. The car had a tiny gear lever hidden away out of sight low down on the driver's right, which meant that when you approached a corner under pressure, you would frantically scrabble about for it in vain, often searching for it on the wrong side of the car altogether. The clutch was very heavy, and was either 'in' or 'out'. It was impossible to slip it, and it was all too easy to stall the engine as you tried to leave the pits.

My sales colleagues drove the car around the track as if they were late for a customer meeting, which being dynamic, they usually were. I drove it around much more sedately, as if I was driving my Morris Marina to a customer meeting I was early for, which not being dynamic, I usually was.

As a final treat, we were taken around the track in a 'hot' Honda hatchback by a racing driver at near racing speeds. We approached the corners at seemingly suicidal speeds, but somehow got around with tyres scrabbling for grip. The car never seemed to be pointing in the direction we were actually travelling. The speed with which the driver's feet pumped the accelerator, clutch and brake was incredible. Funnily enough, I didn't feel carsick, there just wasn't time! I did enjoy it, but I was also quite pleased to tumble out of the car in one piece. All I could smell was hot brakes!

In the distance I can hear a train. It is not a steam train this time, just a fast modern express. A railway bridge crossing the river looms ahead of me. I go under the bridge just as another train passes overhead. As it rumbles over me I pray that the old bridge is still up to supporting the train's massive weight!

So far, my performance on the Ridgeway Challenge has been rather patchy! In 2016, which was my first attempt, I completed it in just under 26 hours. However, the following year I foolishly elected to start at 12 o'clock, which put me under time pressure right from the off. I jogged to Wendover in record time, arriving a full 20 minutes earlier than I had the previous year. It was a hot day and a short time later, while climbing Coombe Hill, I felt unwell and had to pull out. In 2018 things went well until I reached Grim's Ditch. I don't know why, but I just mentally 'caved in' and decided I would stop at Goring where my daughter was waiting to see me go past. In 2019, I was determined to get it right, but again the day was very hot and I set off far too fast. I got as far as Chinnor, but feeling rather faint, I decided to pull out.

I come to a fence barring my way, which forces me to turn left away from the river up a road into the village of South Stoke. I glance at my watch and see that although I am doing alright, there is no way I will be able to maintain a fast enough pace to complete the whole distance in under twenty four hours. I turn right into the high street and walk past a large church on my left. A Race Steward is standing outside a pub, and directs me down a passage to the village hall which is the South Stoke checkpoint. My spirits lift noticeably as I reach the half way point. This is my chance to rest briefly, and get some food inside me. However, as I enter the hall, I am greeted by the smell of food being cooked, which instantly turns my stomach and makes me feel sick. A volunteer tries to encourage me to have something to eat, and enthusiastically reels off a selection of various hot food dishes which they can prepare for me. Swallowing hard, I thank them for their kindness, and quickly explain that sweet coffee and a banana are all my stomach will tolerate for the moment.

South Stoke checkpoint

Arrival time at checkpoint: Saturday 21:26

Stage distance: 7.5 miles
Time taken to complete the stage: 2:16
Average speed for the stage: 3.30 mph

Distance since starting: 41.7 miles
Time taken since starting: 11:22
Average speed since starting: 3.67 mph

Distance left to Avebury: 44.3 miles

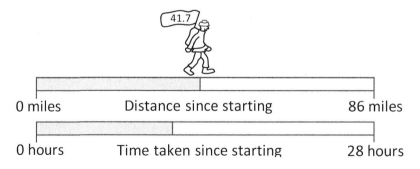

| 0 miles | Distance since starting | 86 miles |

| 0 hours | Time taken since starting | 28 hours |

6 : South Stoke to Bury Down (10.7 miles)

I am well looked after by the volunteers, and set off again with my coffee container full of well-sugared coffee. As I leave the hall and step out into the night it seems to have got a lot chillier during the fifteen minutes that I have been in there. A well-meaning lady, whose expression when she sees me seems to say, 'My God you do look ill!' notes my race number and asks me if I am sure I want to carry on. I smile and assure her that I do, and walk away briskly into the night, feeling slightly desperate and starting to shiver a little. Within half a mile, I am already regretting that I didn't put my extra jumper on under my jacket. "Too late now, too much hassle to stop again in the dark!" I rather stupidly say to myself, and press on. At the southern end of the village I go into fields again, and continue to walk along the bank of the River Thames. The shape of the railway embankment is just discernible to my left. The track morphs into a bumpy private road and I pass several large houses. This continues for about a mile, and then the path rises above the Thames as properties with private moorings start to appear on my right between me and the river.

Seeing the Thames, although it is dark, makes me think about my attempts at paddling kayaks. When my three children were young we all went on a family adventure holiday run by a man called Rob Hastings in Denbigh, North Wales. Rob was famous for having canoed down Everest some years earlier. There was a choice of activities each day, and one day I chose the kayaking option. In the swimming pool, I tried unsuccessfully to master righting an upturned kayak. When they turned my kayak upside down I was quite comfortable with my head underwater, and had no feeling of panic, but I was completely disoriented. Try as I may, I just could not right it myself without an instructor helping me. However, I did became expert at releasing the apron and getting out of the kayak when my breath ran out!

In spite of this, I later bought two second-hand kayaks and took them to the Baiter slipway in Poole Harbour. My older son and I decided that we would try to paddle them around Brownsea Island. Crossing the main shipping lane in the harbour was a bit nerve-wracking, but after that it was a really pleasant trip. An amazing experience for us both that I shall never forget.

I must concentrate here. The road surface is now tarmac, and I spot a Ridgeway Path sign with my torch which directs me across the road and into a narrow unlit alley. The alley takes me between blocks of flats for several hundred yards and emerges onto a road. I am now in the backstreets of Goring. This is the place where my daughter met me on my first Ridgeway Challenge attempt to see how I was getting on. I was in such a state of trance, walking on 'autopilot', that for a couple of minutes I failed to register that it was her, and only after chatting for a while did I realise that this kind young woman talking to me was my daughter! I walk down the road to the high street and turn right. Ahead are the two old bridges that span the River Thames.

While on one of our 'Rob Hastings' holidays, my older son and I learnt the basics of rock climbing and how to use ropes and climbing gear. We went to an escarpment in the Denbigh area with the instructors called World's End where there were lots of single pitch routes of varying difficulty for us to practise on. It was great fun and I learned a lot and gained in confidence.

On one occasion we went off with two instructors to do our first two-pitch climb. This was a whole new experience! One instructor went up, and then my son and I climbed up, protected by the rope, to join him on a ledge half way up the rockface. I remember standing there perched on the ledge, my jacket flapping in the breeze, thinking to myself: "Crikey, this is the real thing!" One instructor climbed above us out of sight and called down when he was at the top. Dry mouthed, I started climbing. I found it hard and felt very exposed, and when I was maybe ten feet above the instructor who was still standing on the ledge below me, I called down to him, "It's no good, I can't go up any farther!" "You jolly well can't come back down!" he shouted back. (I have deleted the expletives in his reply). I remember taking a deep breath, and throwing all caution to the wind, I powered up the remaining part of the climb like a mountain lion. It was pure adrenalin that saved me that day.

After the holiday I bought a climbing rope and some gear, and my son and I went to Little Tryfan, a well-known rock climbing nursery slope in North Wales, to test out our newfound climbing knowledge. I perched on a ledge and spent ten minutes cautiously anchoring myself on to the rock in three places just to be sure. I sat there, ropes all around me, like a fly caught in a spider's web, and called down to my now impatient son, "Climb when ready." He dutifully called back "Climbing." Within ten seconds, at the most, he had effortlessly scrambled up to my position as I tried desperately and unsuccessfully to take in the slack rope through my figure-of-eight. I took several more minutes to disentangle myself from my perch. Needless to say, this did nothing to enhance my rock climbing credentials in my son's eyes. He was clearly a far better climber than me!

I think 'V Diff' grade is definitely my limit for leading, so I won't be tackling El Capitan solo any time soon. However, my limited climbing experience has stood me in good stead because it means I am reasonable at scrambling and know how to use a rope for protection when I am in a group.

As I cross the bridge in Goring looking upriver, I am looking down on a riverside hotel and restaurant. It is ablaze with coloured lights that reflect in the water. I think a wedding reception is taking place. I walk on up the hill to the top of the high street, and turn right at the traffic lights by a pub called The Bull on the other side of the road. After two hundred yards I take the road forking left off the main road, and after another two hundred yards I turn left up a small lane. I follow it going past houses for about one and a half miles, at which point it turns into a rough farm track. I am filled with apprehension about the next stretch of the route. I know this will sound rather melodramatic, but I feel that this is the point where I am leaving civilization behind me and heading up onto the more exposed and isolated North Wessex Downs. For the next six hours or so I will be quite alone as I push on through the hours of darkness. Will my poor old legs take it?

The most dramatic place I have walked has been on the Cuillin hills in Skye. The main Cuillin ridge stretches for over eight miles, and consists of a number of steep bare rocky peaks linked by narrow ridges. Once up on the ridges, there are only certain places where it is possible to make a safe descent. Some of the peaks are rock climbs requiring expertise and the right equipment. Most of the others involve some degree of exposure and require the use of hands as well as feet. It is difficult to decide on adjectives to describe

Main Cuillin Ridge on Skye

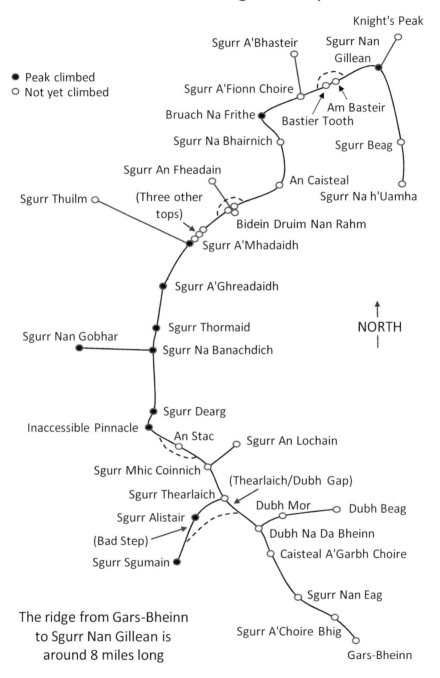

The ridge from Gars-Bheinn
to Sgurr Nan Gillean is
around 8 miles long

the Cuillin Ridge. It is forbidding, beautiful, awesome, stark, challenging, scary and inspiring, all at the same time. Exploits on the peaks must always be properly planned and taken seriously. However, it draws walkers and climbers back to it time after time. It is said that a fit party can traverse the whole ridge end to end in around fourteen hours, and the record is under four hours!

Over the years I have been there five times. However, I would never have gone there if my friend Clive had not suggested that we go, taking my older son with us. We drove up, a distance of around six hundred and twenty five miles, crossing the short stretch of water to Skye on the car ferry because the bridge had not been built then. We stayed quite comfortably in the Youth Hostel at Glenbrittle, which had a large party of Germans staying there. As I was trying to travel light, I had only packed one book to read in the evenings when there was not much to do. Sitting around the table surrounded by all of the foreign voices, I felt slightly awkward because, of all the books I could have brought with me, I had brought one called 'The Story of the Spitfire'.

Our first expeditions took us up Sgurr Nan Gobhar (Scorr Nan Goar), which directly faced the Youth Hostel, and on to Sgurr Na Banachdich to claim our first peak on the main ridge. We also drove around to the Sligachan Hotel, and from there climbed Sgurr Nan Gillean (Scorr Nan Gheel-yan). We followed the so called 'tourist route' up the south east ridge to the summit. We scrambled up the last exposed one hundred feet to reach the small top. The ground all around falls away so steeply that, as you stand there, you feel as if you are suspended in space. After spending some time there, we carried on down the West Ridge until we came to a point which was at the top of Nicholson's Chimney. We abseiled down it, but I suspect you could probably climb down without too much difficulty in dry weather. That was our second peak. In the evening, we went to the Sligachan Hotel for a meal. The bar was crowded with tough looking outdoor characters, and the air was full of strong Scottish accents. Being me, I tried to form a queue at the crowded bar. My turn never seemed to come, but after quite a long wait, the barman took pity on me. I had to speak up because of the background noise. "Half a pint of lager and a Diet Coke please," I said as clearly as possible in my very English slightly cockney accent. The effect was startling. The bar fell silent, rather like in Star Wars when Obi-Wan Kenobi goes into the bar at the Mos Eisley spaceport with Chewbacca. After several seconds, conversations started up again. In fact they turned out to be a friendly crowd.

We had many adventurous expeditions on return visits over the next few years, and we gradually managed to climb quite a number of peaks and started getting to know some sections of the ridge. I was never under any illusion that I would ever be able to achieve the popular challenge of doing the whole ridge from Gars-Bheinn (Garsh-Vain) in the south to Sgurr Nan Gillean in the north. There are several sections along the route where rock climbing skills are essential, and having looked at them, I came to the conclusion that they were well beyond my capability.

However, in some cases it is possible to bypass a difficult section by descending slightly and joining the ridge a little way past the obstruction. I wondered if it might be possible for me to do the ridge taking advantage of these small excursions. However, there are still two sections that would definitely pose problems for me. To avoid climbing the Thearlaich/Dubh (Hyaal-uch/Doo) gap, you have to traverse left to the col between Sgurr Sgumain (Scorr Skoo-men) and Sgurr Alistair. Once at the col, as you turn right and ascend towards Sgurr Alistair, the ridge narrows, and you come to a rock wall barring the way called the Bad Step. It is only about ten feet high, but has awkward out-of-balance sloping holds, and is definitely not the place to injure yourself! Provided you can overcome it, you can easily go over Sgurr Alistair and then descend to the top of the Great Stone Shoot. It is then a hard scramble onto Thearlaich.

Another problem area, which is still a mystery to me, is the three northern tops of Sgurr A'Mhadaidh (Scorr A'Vha-ty). The southern top is just a scramble, but you cannot bypass the three northern tops which are more difficult. The biggest problem I have found when I am walking in unfamiliar terrain for the first time is that you can do your research in a guide book, but you can't really judge if you are capable of scrambling over an obstacle until you actually try to. My fear is that I will scramble up a rockface, only to *find that it becomes too difficult, and when I try to retreat I find that I can't! As a result, the aim of several of our walks was to reconnoitre and get to know sections of the ridge, while the whole time erring on the cautious side so as not to get into difficulty in such an unforgiving environment.*

On one occasion, we left the Youth Hostel and ascended the gigantic corrie called Coir' a' Ghrunnda. Once high up, we were able to climb onto the col between Sgurr Sgumain and Sgurr Alistair. We scrambled up to the famous Bad Step, which my son was able to climb successfully. Protected by a rope that he lowered to me, and assisted by a bit of a pull from him, I joined him and we scrambled on up the narrowing ridge to the airy summit of Sgurr Alistair. It is the highest peak on Skye, and as the weather was warm and clear, the views were magnificent.

Another memorable outing was when we ascended to Sgurr Dearg (Scorr Jerrack), and then managed to walk and scramble all the way to the most southerly top of Sgurr A'Mhadaidh. This involved lots of exciting scrambling, and several sections of the route were very exposed, particularly as we negotiated the knife edge ridge between the twin tops of Sgurr A'Ghreadaidh (Scorr A'Gret-a).

From the southern top of Sgurr A'Mhadaidh, we could see the three more northerly tops, and they looked rather intimidating. Crossing them would involve climbing, and possibly some abseiling as well. Beyond them, we glimpsed the three tops of Bidean Druim Nan Rahm (Bidyan-Drim-Nan-Rahv), and they looked even more challenging. We decided to call it a day, so retraced our footsteps as far as An Dorus. We then left the ridge altogether, and descended to the Youth Hostel feeling rather pleased with ourselves.

The wide chalky track climbs steadily up a hill gaining quite a lot of height in the next couple of miles. About five miles out of Goring another track crosses mine, and I turn right onto it. It is a single-lane track for farm vehicles with a smooth concreted surface. I slowly gain more height as the track bends to the left. I can hear the sound of traffic coming from some way off. The wind picks up and the temperature continues to drop. The concrete surface goes on for around another one and a half miles.

On my second visit to Skye, I was with my sixteen year old son and my friend Clive. Back at home prior to the trip I had sat in an armchair in front of a roaring fire, thumbing through my Poucher book on the Scottish Peaks. Over a period of years, some walkers try to 'bag' all of the two hundred and seventy seven peaks in Scotland that are over three thousand feet high, which appear in a list compiled by a man called Sir Hugh Monro. One Munro peak turns out to be a major problem for walkers who are not accustomed to scrambling or climbing. The problem peak is Sgurr Dearg in

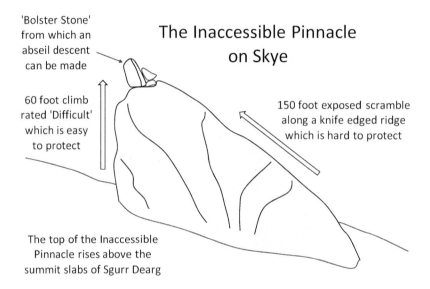

'Bolster Stone' from which an abseil descent can be made

The Inaccessible Pinnacle on Skye

60 foot climb rated 'Difficult' which is easy to protect

150 foot exposed scramble along a knife edged ridge which is hard to protect

The top of the Inaccessible Pinnacle rises above the summit slabs of Sgurr Dearg

the Cuillins, where the tip of a shaft of rock sprouting from just below the summit, called The Inaccessible Pinnacle, is actually higher than the summit itself. From the comfort and security of my chair at home, I looked at photographs of it in the book which were taken from all angles, and convinced myself that it didn't look too hard after all. "What's all the fuss about?" I naively thought.

Standing beside the real thing was an entirely different proposition. It was much bigger than I had expected and the two ways of climbing it both looked really daunting. The East Ridge had a gentler sloping aspect involving a scramble along a long exposed knife edge which looked difficult to protect with a rope. I had visions of coming off half way along and swinging into the abyss like a pendulum until I contacted sold rock at high speed. The alternative route up the West Ridge was definitely more than a scramble and required the protection of a rope. After thinking about it for a few nanoseconds, I discounted the scramble along the East ridge. I just wasn't brave enough for that. Fortunately, as my son was a good climber, we agreed that he would lead up the steeper West Ridge and I would follow him. Clive volunteered to look after the rucksacks and call Mountain Rescue if I got stuck part of the way up. My son made the climb look easy. I belayed him as he climbed up to the 'Bolster Stone' perched at the top and tied himself on. Dry-mouthed, I followed him protected by the rope, removing the various bits of gear and slings he had left on his way up, and joined him at the top. Surprisingly, it was not as difficult as I had feared. There were plenty of good holds, and the rock was dry that day which made it easier. Clive took some great photographs of the two of us at the top as we posed for the camera. We had done it!

Getting back down was just a matter of abseiling from a large karabiner that was attached to a stout wire looped around the Bolster Stone. As I abseiled down the rockface, I remember gazing straight up at the Bolster Stone above me, and wondering just how many thousands of years it had been precariously perched up there. It occurred to me that one day it would have eroded just enough for it to topple off, and I started praying that this was not the day in question. Looking on the bright side, I figured that it must weigh several tons, so if it fell on me it would all be over very quickly. Also, as a bonus, it would be the only way that I would ever become famous in rock climbing circles. I could just imagine the sort of sensational headlines that might appear about my mishap in the press:

- *Flattened father of three hailed as hero*
- *"He's felt squashed all his life so it's how he would have wanted to go." says climber's wife*
- *Mountain Rescue ferry climber off hardest Monro on four stretchers*
- *Beastly Bolster brains brave backpacker*
- *Skye climbing tragedy - SNP spokesperson says Tory cuts to blame*

The sound of traffic becomes much louder, and I can see lights from the cars speeding along the A34 some distance ahead. They are closer now, and going downhill I reach a small tunnel that takes the track under the A34. There is a Bronze Age Round Barrow somewhere along here just off the track, but I expect I will miss it in the dark. I am surprised that there is so much traffic at this time of night. The minds and bodies of elite athletes are honed to such a high degree that they can pick up the first subtle sign in their bodies that fatigue is setting in. In my case, when I am getting tired, the sign is less subtle. I just keep tripping over, and when I look back, I can't see what it was I tripped up on. I am starting to gain height again and the track is becoming more grassy. After about half a mile I can see a light in the field ahead. I arrive at the Bury Down checkpoint which has been set up in a small car park. I am so impressed by the cheerful volunteers who greet me. They must have been waiting for many hours on this chilly hillside for runners to arrive, and it's now after midnight. The event would not be possible without their dedication.

Bury Down checkpoint

Arrival time at checkpoint:	Sunday 00:56
Stage distance:	10.7 miles
Time taken to complete the stage:	3:30
Average speed for the stage:	3.06 mph
Distance since starting:	52.4 miles
Time taken since starting:	14:52
Average speed since starting:	3.52 mph
Distance left to Avebury:	33.6 miles

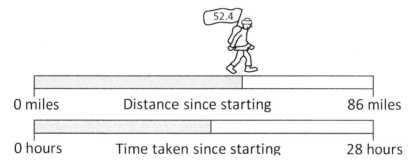

0 miles	Distance since starting	86 miles

0 hours	Time taken since starting	28 hours

7 : Bury Down to Sparsholt Firs (9.1 miles)

I top up my water bottle and leave almost straight away. The chalk track is less distinct for a while, and then becomes deeply rutted. I must keep a sharp look out for a large monument which should appear on my left after roughly one hour's walking.

Maybe my distant ancestors were bowmen at Agincourt, or even game keepers on a large country estate. This sounds fanciful, but it came as a complete revelation to me when I discovered that I am a good shot with both a bow and arrow and a shotgun.

On holiday, I had the chance to fire a proper bow and arrow at a target for the first time, and I was uncannily accurate. The whole process of aiming and firing just seemed so natural to me. I didn't have to take precise aim squinting along the arrow, I just took in the whole scene in front of me and felt I was on target, and then loosed the arrow.

At work, I went on a team building afternoon clay pigeon shooting, and never having fired a gun before in my life, I was amazed to find I was able to hit the moving clay targets. Not just one target, but two targets moving in the opposite direction to each other. Again, I didn't have to take careful aim looking along the barrel, there just wasn't time to do that anyway. I just sort of poked the gun at a point in the sky ahead of the target, and squeezed. I'm relieved that in my lifetime I have never been called up into the armed forces as my ancestors were, and put into a 'kill or be killed' situation, forcing me to use my skill with a gun.

However, I can claim no special talent when it comes to dingy sailing. I taught myself to sail an Enterprise by reading the Ladybird Book of Dingy Sailing. I was able to master making it go in all directions, and to understand the mysteries of the centreboard, but when my friend and I entered it in a competition on a large lake somewhere near Bedford, we disgraced ourselves by capsizing it near the start line! I once went out in a dingy with a work colleague who lived in Portsmouth who was an expert sailor. I couldn't relax and enjoy the experience because he never sat still in the boat for an instant. He continually jumped about in it from side to side, violently wrenching the tiller back and forth and adjusting this and that. He was so competitive! There was absolutely no pleasure in it at all for me.

I acquired a second hand Topper dingy, and took it down to Poole Harbour. With my younger son who was about ten years old at the time, we set off to sail anticlockwise around Brownsea Island. He has never forgiven me for the experience that I made him endure that day. All went well as we set off from the Baiter slipway and made our way across the main shipping channel. We successfully went around the northern tip of the island and stayed close to the coast until we arrived at the southwest tip, opposite the harbour entrance.

That is where things went wrong. I tried to come around the bottom of the island, but I was then heading directly into the wind. At the same time the tide was rushing out towards the harbour mouth, and the result was that however hard I tried to tack, I just lost ground the whole time and was carried nearer and nearer to the harbour mouth and the open sea. After about half an hour of tacking, I gave up and we returned clockwise around the island, back the way we had come. I thoroughly enjoyed it, even though we didn't make it all the way around the island. My son, who hadn't wanted to accompany me in the first place, hated every moment, and even now over twenty five years later frequently reminds me of what I put him through.

I come to a point where the track forks and I take the left fork. There are not many landmarks visible along this stretch of the track. Suddenly I see the monument on my left, so I must be on the right path. It's about forty feet tall, and my torch picks out the cross at the very top. It was erected in memory of Baron Wantage by his wife. I'd like to stop, but there is no time to have a proper look now. I must try to do this part of the route in daylight so that I get a chance to see what is actually around me.

It was pitch black and I was aware that my whole world had shrunk into a small bubble. It extended only as far as I could see, hear, smell and touch. In the light from my torch I could only see a little of the track ahead, I could hear my own breathing and footsteps, I could smell the pine trees, and I could feel the breeze on my face and the sharp flints in the chalk path through my shoes. Suddenly my mobile phone rang, startling me and bringing me back to reality. I had arranged for my son, who was working a night shift in London, to phone me a couple of times for a chat. I fumbled with the torch and phone, trying to unlock the phone so that I could chat. I found it difficult without my reading glasses. I had wondered how good reception would be so far from built up areas, but it turned out to be very good, because I was high up on a hill I suppose. His voice was quite clear, as if we were standing in the same room.

I think mobile phones are amazing devices, and I have never taken radio, television or telephones for granted. They still seem a bit mysterious and miraculous to me. It is just as well we can only see a small range of electronic radiation in the form of visible light. If we could see the TV and mobile phone transmissions as well, which saturate the air around us the whole time, surely we would be completely overwhelmed and blinded by their dazzling intensity.

Two more runners pass me and their little bubble of light quickly disappears into the darkness some distance ahead. By now, I am guessing that the whole field of runners has overtaken me, and that I am now last. Dozens have gone by me, one by one or in small groups, and I am sure that a number of runners will have pulled out of the event at various checkpoints along the way. As the runners passed me, I saw that many of them were festooned with lights, and wired up with elaborate looking communication devices of all sorts which they were talking into.

I reflected on how different things are now compared to when I was young. In modern life we have grown accustomed to an individual walking towards us, ignoring us completely while apparently talking to themselves in a loud voice. How times have changed! In my day, if you walked along the road talking to yourself out loud, you would be grabbed and locked up!

Some time ago, I was travelling in a train into London, when from somewhere far down the carriage came the penetrating voice of an elderly lady talking on her mobile phone. The rest of the train fell silent as we were all forced to listen to her conversation. Her half of the conversation went something like this:

"No, Bill's fine, but last week he noticed it was still getting bigger."

"No, they told him it would be better to have it out and be done with it."

"I know, he was booked in to get it sorted next Thursday, but it burst."

"No, they say they can't take the other two out until sometime next year."

I and my fellow passengers sat transfixed, desperately trying to work out what Bill's problem could possibly be. At that point in the conversation I arrived at my station. As I brushed past the man sitting next to me he smiled and quietly said, "Too much information!" I often think of Bill and wonder if he has had the other two out yet, or if either of them have burst as well before he got the chance. What on earth could Bill have had three of anyway?

On TV, back in the 1960s there was a series called 'The Man from U.N.C.L.E.' about secret agents. The heroes each had communications devices that looked like fountain pens which they could whip out when they were in an impossible situation to call for backup. It all seemed so futuristic and impossible back then. Modern mobiles can do far more impressive things than those secret agents' pens ever could.

It is amazing how many of the plots of films made before the 1980s would fall apart if the characters in the film had had mobile phones. Usually, the police inspector sends one of his men off to find a phone box so that he can phone the 'Yard' to warn them, while in the meantime the villains get clean away! If the inspector had had a mobile phone the film would have been much shorter, because it would have been over after the first five minutes.

I should be passing an old hill fort called Segsbury Castle on my right about now, but I can't see anything in the dark. I seem to have been walking for ages since the last checkpoint, and I reckon I still have quite a way to go before I get to the Sparsholt Firs checkpoint. I am finding it very difficult to keep track of time as I plod on for several miles along the dark featureless track. I have been to Sparsholt Firs in daylight and I try to picture where I am right now and what I would be seeing. A large clump of pine trees stands at the top of a hill, and as you approach, you can see them while you are still a long way off. On the right just before you get there the grassy slopes fall steeply away into a deep hollow called the Devil's Punchbowl.

One of the best walks I have done was with my son on Ben Nevis when he was about fifteen years old. As we started our walk from the A82 through a golf course, there was a lot of snow lying on the higher slopes. We walked up the valley by a line of lovely rowan trees growing on a river bank, and then veered off to the left, climbing steeply onto a ridge.

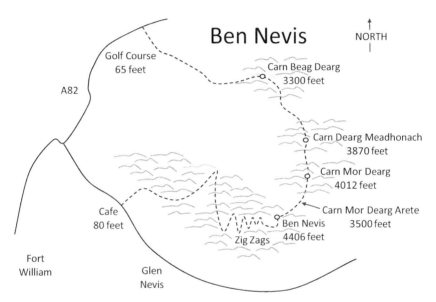

We traversed the ridge from peak to peak with wonderful views of Ben Nevis on our right the whole time. We descended to the arete and started the stiff scramble up the rocks to the summit. Unfortunately, the top was enveloped in thick cloud so we saw nothing of the view. We crossed the small snow covered summit plateau, and descended by the so-called tourist route, initially down the zig-zags, and then on down a rough winding track to the cafe.

I returned to Ben Nevis many years later in very different circumstances. Over previous years, I had entered the Snowdon Race in Wales several times, running from Llanberis along a rough track next to the railway line up to the Snowdon summit, and then back down again. The distance is around five miles in each direction, and the height gain is about three thousand feet. The ascent is unrelenting, steeper in some places than others, but with an average gradient of one in eight. I remember that I used to meet the leading runners coming down just after I had passed Halfway House on my way up! It was easy to trip on the rough track, and on one occasion when I was nearly down, I tripped while running quite fast. When you are descending at a pace, you have so much forward momentum that there is not enough time to adjust your other foot to regain your balance. Miraculously, because when I fall I tend to roll over and over rather than just crash into the ground, I escaped with a few minor grazes. Several other runners were not so lucky, and went past me with their faces and shirts covered in blood.

My thoughts turned to what it would be like to run up Ben Nevis in a similar fashion. There is an organised event, but the entry is limited, and the event seemed to be geared towards elite runners rather than me. I decided to have a go on my own. With some ingenuity I persuaded my wife that it was about time we had a holiday in Scotland, and suggested that Fort William would make a jolly good base.

The caravan we rented was about four miles from Fort William, so with my tracksuit trousers and jacket on over my running gear, I set off walking towards Fort William with my wife. When we got to Glen Nevis, she turned right into Fort William, armed with her debit card for a shopping spree, and I walked up the Glen to the café and car park. There, I stripped down to my shorts and running gear, and put my clothes into my rucksack with my hat, gloves and other supplies.

I ran up the initially steep rocky path until the gradient eased. After some time I branched off sharply to the right. I only met a couple of parties as I went. As I climbed the zig-zags, high above me, I could see the boundary where the cloud started. I met a Ranger coming towards me who had just been to the summit. He was aghast that I was heading up with so little clothing. I explained that I had all sorts of extra clothing in my rucksack and assured him that I would be fine. I left him shaking his head, and no doubt thinking *that he would be a member of the rescue party when it was called out for me sometime in the next few hours.*

As I approached the cloud boundary the air chilled dramatically. Suddenly there was deep soft snow underfoot, which I sunk in almost up to my knees. The air filled with driving sleet as I pushed on a short distance until I arrived at the first of the tall marker stones near the summit. I decided I had better stop and put on all of my spare clothing. I had to take my shoes off before I could put my trousers on, and I then quickly donned my trousers, pullover, and hat and laid my gloves down ready to put on. I put my shoes back on, but by then my fingers were so bitterly cold that I couldn't do up the laces. I left the laces undone, pulled on my gloves and pressed on to the next marker stone which was barely visible through flurries of snow.

Visibility was getting worse and worse, and I started to get worried because I knew that at one point, I had to take a sharp left turn from one marker to the next to arrive safely at the summit. If I missed the turn and carried straight on I would be in danger because I would be heading directly down a notorious gully. Relieved, I spotted the turn and knew the old observatory on the summit must now be no more than one hundred and fifty yards ahead of me. I congratulated myself for doing my homework before my run.

After exchanging a few words with a party at the summit, I carefully retraced my footsteps until I was below the snowline once again. All the time I had been on the move I had stayed tolerably warm, but I can see how quickly hyperthermia would have set in if I had been injured and unable to move. With all my clothing on I powered on down the slopes, feeling warmer and warmer as I got lower and lower. I was really chuffed that I had managed to do it.

Safely back down at the café, I soberly reflected on the experience. I acknowledged to myself that it was not at all like me to take such risks, and promised myself I would learn from the experience. I'd had no backup plan if things had gone wrong. I didn't even have a mobile with me. I had a plastic survival bag, map, compass, whistle, torch and food but I don't think I would have lasted for long if I had got into trouble anywhere on the mountain above the half way point.

I walked thoughtfully back to our caravan where my wife was waiting with her purchases, among which was a half-bottle of Brandy which she knows I like in coffee. She is so good to me! When she asked me how it had gone, I said it had gone fine, but had been a bit chilly at the top. I glossed over the riskier aspects of my adventure. It had been a stimulating experience, but without wishing to be too dramatic, I felt that I had acted recklessly and must surely have used up one of my nine lives.

Farther up the hill I can see a light. I'm not sure what it is because according to my GPS watch, I reckon I still have another three miles to go before I get to Sparsholt Firs. However, my watch seems to have under-read the distance by three miles. What a welcome surprise! When I ask the lady who greets me if this is the Sparsholt Firs checkpoint, she gives me an odd look as if to say, "Where else could it possibly be? There's nothing for miles around in all directions!" Several runners are already there, seated in a large tent, all looking cold and rather dejected.

Sparsholt checkpoint

Arrival time at checkpoint:	Sunday 03:53
Stage distance:	9.1 miles
Time taken to complete the stage:	2:57
Average speed for the stage:	3.08 mph
Distance since starting:	61.5 miles
Time taken since starting:	17:49
Average speed since starting:	3.45 mph
Distance left to Avebury:	24.5 miles

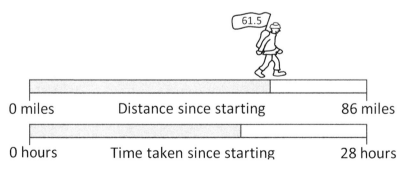

0 miles	Distance since starting	86 miles

0 hours	Time taken since starting	28 hours

8 : Sparsholt Firs to Foxhill (7.9 miles)

My large coffee mug is filled up, and I put in two lumps of sugar. There is no time to stop, so I set off gingerly sipping at it because it is so hot. I leave the runners seated in the tent who, having retired from the event, are now waiting for a lift to Avebury. The track is rough and chalky, and seems to be never-ending. Will I ever get there? I cheer myself up by saying, "Oh well, only a marathon distance to go!" Once again I am passing a major landmark that I can't see. On my right is another ancient earthwork called Uffington Castle Fort, thought to have been built as long ago as the 7th century. I can see it only as a dark shape on the horizon. Beyond will be the famous White Horse carved on the other side of the hill. At night, the time passing between checkpoints is difficult to estimate, probably because you can see so little of the landscape and so few landmarks. Most of the time, all you have is your thoughts, and as fatigue and sleep deprivation takes its toll, I start to think depressing thoughts about life itself.

I picture us as just one of many species trying to survive on our planet, an oasis in the airless void of space. For most creatures, life is just a matter of trying to avoid predators who are after you for their next meal. For even top predators like us, life is a battle against parasites and viruses with our immune systems constantly battling to stop them invading our bodies and getting the upper hand.

Our bodies are really just vehicles for transporting our brains about the place and ensuring they have a good supply of nutrients. We seem to waste such a large part of our lives sleeping to restore our bodies, or cooking and eating food to fuel our bodies and keep them functioning. However, we are fortunate that modern technology frees us from the constant pressure to go out hunting for food, and enables us to spend our time much more profitably doing really productive things, like watching 'Celebrity Gogglebox' on TV.

I've always had an unshakeable belief that I exist just behind my eyes, from where I view the events occurring in the ever changing world in my vicinity. What a tiny sphere of reality I am experiencing the whole time though, and by the time I have processed and digested the images I see, the information is already out of date. Reality has moved on. I am always behind the curve, struggling to keep up.

What a miracle life is! I take my hat off to Mother Nature who has built living creatures out of the most unpromising materials. She doesn't have metal, plastic, glass, glue, oil, petrol or cement to work with. It's an incredible thought that if I do make it all the way to Avebury, the bones, tendons and muscles in my legs, fuelled by a constant blood supply, will have taken over 170,000 steps without a break to transport the rest of my carcass there!

As I walk on in silence, I feel as if I am gradually melting into the landscape that surrounds me and becoming part of it. I feel a connection with it that I have only experienced a handful of times before when walking alone in North Wales. It's a shame that back in the 1960s, the poor old Beatles had to trek all the way to Tibet to search for a similar 'transcendental experience'. After all, in reality all I am is just a clump of molecules that have been temporarily assembled from handy bits and pieces that were lying around, and one day those molecules will all go their own separate ways again. This is starting to depress me, so I pull myself together and snap out of it. One mile further on I am brought back to reality again as my torch picks out a sign pointing off to the right to Wayland Smithy. This is a Neolithic burial chamber that was built before the Pyramids! I really must visit here at a more sensible time during the day! I drink my remaining half-bottle of Lucozade which goes down well and makes me feel a little better.

One summer, I went to Glen Coe in Scotland. As you drive down the valley on the A82 towards Fort William, to your right is an impressive jagged ridge named the Aonach Eagach. It is one of the finest knife-edged ridge challenges in the UK. To your left are three peaks known as the Three Sisters of Glen Coe. They form part of the Bidean range, and from the road they hide several even higher peaks which lie behind them.

I camped at the bottom of the glen, and walked up the path by the road until I was opposite Am Bodach. It was a misty morning, and as I ascended the scree to its right, I could only see fifty yards ahead of me. When I reached the top, I had to carefully climb down fifty feet on its western side on polished rock to get onto the narrow ridge. The impressive ridge snaked out in front of me, disappearing into the mist, and the ground plummeted away steeply on either side. I felt as if I was suspended high up in a cloud. It was an exciting place to walk as I traversed from peak to peak, scrambling over one pinnacle after another that barred the way. The really challenging part of the scramble lasted for about the first two miles, and then the going got easier.

Once on the ridge, you have to continue for a long while before you can descend safely. You pass a slightly chilling sign that warns you not to attempt to descend from the ridge until you have reached Sgorr nam Fiannaidh. I knew from looking at the map beforehand that this was the name of one of the peaks, but in the mist, which one was it? How would I recognise it when I got there? Slightly rattled by the sign, I pressed on knowing that if the worst came to the worst, if I stayed on the ridge for long enough, I would eventually walk safely off to low ground, although I would end up a long way from my campsite.

Glen Coe

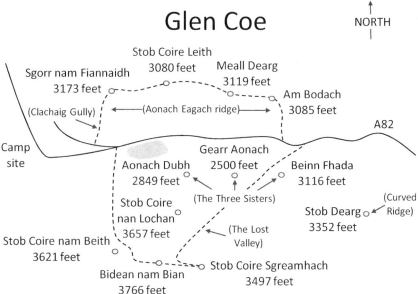

↑
NORTH
|

I came to a point where it looked safe to descend to my left, and started down the scree, losing quite a lot of height. It was raining hard, and I felt cold and tired. The ground got steeper and steeper, and I began to fear that I had descended too early and may come to the top of a cliff. With

69

great difficulty, I persuaded myself to turn around and climb all the way back up to the ridge. It was so tempting to just carry on descending, but I turned and slogged back up the scree. In fact, I had descended far less than I thought I had, and I was soon back on the crest of the ridge. How your mind can play tricks on you and distort your ability to estimate time and distance when you are tired and worried!

I continued a little further along the ridge, and the rain eased. I arrived at the top of a rough track that descended steeply, winding down to my left. This turned out to be the track just to the west of Clachaig Gully. It was a long descent, and at times the steep track snaked very close to large vertical drops into the gully itself. I carefully picked my way down, trying not to dislodge loose rocks into the gully. Eventually I ended up at a small road by the Youth Hostel. I walked back to my campsite, looking forward to making myself a cup of tea. It had been quite an adventure.

Back at the campsite, I talked to the guy in the next tent who was camping with his girlfriend. He asked me where I had been walking, and seemed quite impressed when I said I had walked along the Aonach Eagach ridge. The couple very kindly offered me some of their hot curry, and then they went to bed early. I had the impression that he was planning a long romantic night of passion, but judging from the noises emanating from their tent, in the end it only lasted for about twenty seconds or so.

The next day, I set off to explore the Bidean range of peaks. Thick cloud covered the tops as I walked up the road from the campsite. I turned right onto the track and climbed for around an hour. Eventually, I could make out the ridge line in front of me through the mist. Suddenly, the mist cleared, and to my left I could see the massive buttresses of Bidean nam Bian, the highest peak in the range. It was an impressive sight, and the sheer scale of my surroundings made me feel completely insignificant. Once on the connecting ridge, I turned left towards the summit of Bidean, but the clouds rolled in again. I was disappointed not to be able to look across from the summit at the Aonach Eagach ridge that I had traversed the previous day. I didn't hang around there for long because there was a chill wind blowing.

I pressed on eastwards, descending at first, and then going uphill again to the summit of Stob Coire Sgreamhach. I had left a note at the campsite describing the route I would be taking, which involved turning back at this point. I knew I had to stick to my plan in case I got into any difficulty. I noticed out of interest that the ground ahead dropped away very steeply, so scrambling any further along the ridge to the east would have been too hard for me in any case.

I returned about halfway towards Bidean, and then turned right, dropping down a short, surprisingly muddy section of scree to the flat floor of a corrie called The Lost Valley. It was one of the most atmospheric places I have ever been. The floor of the corrie is like a giant shelf nestling high up between the mountains either side. When you look ahead, the corrie is flat for some distance and then drops steeply down to the road in the glen, which is out of sight.

In the late 17th century, Glen Coe was the site of a great slaughter, when the people living in the area were attacked. According to legend, some three hundred men, women and children fled into The Lost Valley to escape. They were chased as they sought refuge by running away into the mountains. The place has an eerie brooding feel about it, and I was glad to cross it and descend back down to the road. For the last mile or so, I was attacked mercilessly by midges which had not bothered me at all earlier in the day.

As I arrived back at the campsite, I had enjoyed the day immensely, and my only regret was that visibility had been so poor, and I had not been able to see the many spectacular views of the mountains of Glen Coe.

On my last day, I went along to the eastern end of the glen until I was on the A82 opposite Stob Dearg. There are a string of four tops along a high ridge which is called the Buachaille Etive Mor. Stob Dearg is the highest of the four peaks, and is a well-known place for challenging climbing routes. It also has one sensational scrambling route called Curved Ridge, which although exposed, has good holds.

I crossed the stream, and started ascending the lower slopes of Stob Dearg. As I looked over my shoulder across *the vast expanse of Rannoch Moor, in the distance I could see rain showers approaching. I managed to get about half way up the mountain, almost to where Curved Ridge begins, before the arrival of heavy rain. Visibility was deteriorating rapidly as two climbers caught up with me. I asked them if I was at the point that Curved Ridge began. One of them, in his early twenties, produced a crumpled postcard with a picture of the mountain on it. He pointed out a feature on the mountain as the rain poured down, making the postcard more and more sodden. They then set off, and soon disappeared above me in the mist. I decided that two youngsters using a soggy postcard as a map were probably not the most reliable 'guides' to follow, so I retreated back down the mountain to my car. I felt disappointed that I had not had a proper shot at it.*

I can just detect a faint glow on the horizon behind me as I walk in a westerly direction, the first sign of dawn. The Earth has spun almost half a turn since I first switched on my torch. In the morning light, I can start to make out the dark shapes of trees and bushes around me. I decide to put my torch away, and wince as I am reminded of my attempts to write poetry many years ago. However hard I tried, my poems always turned out to be tortured, over-dramatic and over-ripe. This is the first verse of my rather ambitious poem entitled 'Identity'. I will spare you the other fifteen verses because they are just too harrowing (and embarrassing).

I stir into the morning light,
Today who will I be?
Faced with endless choices,
I choose the same old me.

The ground is rough with flints embedded in the chalk. I catch my toe on one and stumble forward. It's a bad surface to fall on, so I must take care. I chuckle to myself as it reminds me of a joke that brilliant comedian Paul Merton told on TV. He was on a tour of Nelson's flagship when the tour guide stopped and pointed to a plaque fixed to the floor. "That's where Nelson fell," the guide said solemnly. "I'm not surprised, I nearly tripped over it myself," Paul replied. I stow my torch and have a drink. Annoyingly, I find myself endlessly singing over and over again one of the jingles from a 1950s TV advert that brainwashed my whole generation! It promoted Esso Blue Paraffin, and had dodgy grammar to make it rhyme. It was sung to the tune of 'Smoke gets in your eyes'.

They asked me how I knew,
It was Esso Blue,
I of course replies,
With other grades one buys,
Smoke gets in your eyes.

I plod on for about four more miles. The track starts going uphill and I really notice the gradient. I go over the crest of the hill and at last, there ahead of me is the Foxhill checkpoint. As I arrive, I am greeted with a cheery, "Well done, you only have sixteen miles to go!" I have a cup of tea and a banana, but I am really feeling the strain now. I still can't eat anything else, and it is a real fight to keep going. I daren't stop and rest though because I'm afraid I would seize up physically and mentally and I wouldn't be able to get moving again. I feel that the Foxhill checkpoint is a key milestone in the event, and force myself to mentally focus on pushing on to the next checkpoint. If I can just make it to Barbury Castle, there will only be six more miles to the finish.

Foxhill checkpoint

Arrival time at checkpoint: Sunday 06:28

Stage distance: 7.9 miles
Time taken to complete the stage: 2:35
Average speed for the stage: 3.06 mph

Distance since starting: 69.4 miles
Time taken since starting: 20:24
Average speed since starting: 3.40 mph

Distance left to Avebury: 16.6 miles

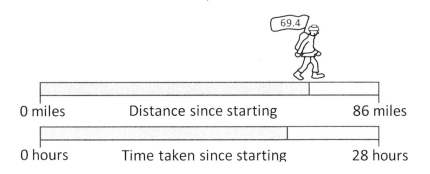

0 miles   Distance since starting   86 miles

0 hours   Time taken since starting   28 hours

9 : Foxhill to Barbury Castle (10.5 miles)

The rough path goes downhill for half a mile to a road. I turn left onto it and walk on the grass verge on the right because there are no pavements. After about half a mile I come to the M4 motorway and cross it over the bridge. More uphill to a junction where I turn left. It's all starting to seem a bit of a dream now. Even though it's light I can still see the Moon. I am always surprised that so many people don't seem to understand or care how it is possible for an object like the Moon to keep orbiting around the Earth month after month. In my experience, if you do try to start an interesting discussion with somebody about orbital dynamics, their reaction is usually to dismiss you as a geek, and to terminate the conversation immediately. As they walk away, I often hear them mumbling: "I don't do maths!"

Many of us look at a painting or statue and see beauty, or go outdoors and look at a landscape and are touched by the beauty we see there. However, fewer people seem to appreciate the sheer beauty of the laws of nature. I can't understand how anyone can fail to marvel at the way that a few simple rules can interact to produce the wonderfully complex motion of the objects we see around us.

The former we label 'art', and the latter we label 'physics', but I think they can both be a source of great beauty and wonder in their own way. Maybe it's just the label 'physics' that puts some people off from making an effort to understand and build up their own picture of what is going on around them.

We live in a technological age when our planet is surrounded by hundreds of artificial satellites that have been put into orbit around it. They have been put there for many different purposes related to: the weather, telephone and TV communications, the military, and investigating climate change. Some of them are even manned. They play a major part in our modern world, and yet not many people seem to understand what keeps them up there swinging around our planet year after year with no engine to keep them moving. If that's not miraculous I don't know what is!

Most of us have at some time tied a weight to a piece of string and swung it around in a circle. The laws of nature say

74

that, if you increase the speed of a circling object you will increase the pull on the string and if you decrease its speed you will decrease the pull on the string. Also, if you suddenly lengthen the string the pull on the string will be less and the weight will circle at a slower speed, and if you shorten the string the pull on the string will be more and the weight will circle at a faster speed.

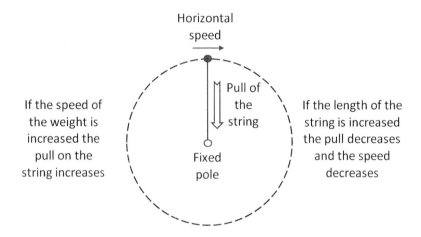

Horizontal speed

Pull of the string

If the speed of the weight is increased the pull on the string increases

Fixed pole

If the length of the string is increased the pull decreases and the speed decreases

Exactly the same laws apply in the case of a satellite. If you want a satellite to stay in a circular orbit at a height of say two hundred kilometres above the Earth, it simply has to be given the exact horizontal speed necessary for the pull of gravity at that height to keep pulling it in a circle. The pull of gravity is acting like an invisible string.

Another important law of nature says that the pull of gravity gets less as you get further from the Earth and more as you get closer to it. This means that the horizontal speed needed for a circular orbit will vary, depending on the height you want the orbit to be. The higher the orbit required, the lower the horizontal speed needed, and the lower the orbit required, the higher the horizontal speed needed.

Provided you get the horizontal speed absolutely spot on for the height of the satellite, the pull and the speed will be 'matched' and the satellite will continue to circle the Earth at that height without the need for any propulsion. How fantastic is that? Of course, you will need a rocket to get the satellite to the right height and to give it the precise 'matching' horizontal speed in the first place.

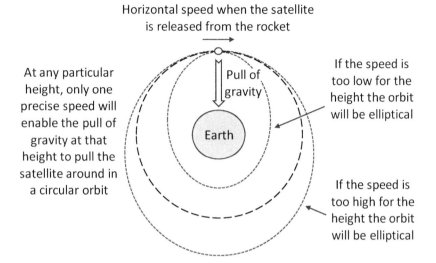

Horizontal speed when the satellite is released from the rocket

Pull of gravity

Earth

At any particular height, only one precise speed will enable the pull of gravity at that height to pull the satellite around in a circular orbit

If the speed is too low for the height the orbit will be elliptical

If the speed is too high for the height the orbit will be elliptical

The real beauty of the interacting laws shows up in cases where the horizontal speed is not perfectly matched to the height. If a satellite's speed when released from a rocket is too fast, the pull of gravity will not be strong enough to keep the orbit circular and the satellite will gain some vertical speed and therefore height. The effect of gaining height is that the pull of gravity will lessen, and the horizontal speed will drop. However, as the height continues to increase, the pull needed to maintain a circular orbit at the new horizontal speed lessens at a higher rate than the drop in the pull of gravity. This means that the upward speed will eventually slow to a halt, and the satellite will then start to descend. The whole process then plays out in reverse. As the height of the satellite decreases, the pull of gravity increases, and the horizontal speed also increases. The result of this interplay between height and horizontal speed is that instead of a nice circular orbit, the shape of the orbit becomes an ellipse. The satellite rises higher in the first half of its orbit, and then plunges back down in the second half of its orbit, before rising up again as it starts its next orbit. If a rocket releases a satellite into orbit with a horizontal speed that is far too slow, it will crash into the Earth. If it's far too fast, it will rush off in a very elongated ellipse, and if it's going fast enough, even escape from the pull of the Earth altogether.

In 1957, I was eleven years old when the first artificial satellite was put into orbit by Russia. I remember my feeling of satisfaction when I managed to work out for myself what kept the satellite circling around up there without an engine to power it. Ever since, I have marvelled at how a few simple rules working together can explain their complicated motion.

About two hundred yards up the road I turn right into an enormous field. The path goes uphill as far as I can see. Near the top of the hill the path veers to the left and levels out again. On my right is yet another hill fort called Liddington Hill Fort. I now have a different tune going around and around in my head that I can't get rid of. It was from the Brylcreem advert. Brylcreem was the deadly stuff that my dad would plaster on my nice clean hair before we left home to visit relatives. The tune went like this:

> *Brylcreem, a little dab'll do yer,*
> *Brylcreem, you'll look so debonair,*
> *Brylcreem, a little dab'll do yer,*
> *She'll love to run her fingers through your hair.*

Today, it just sounds like sexist nonsense, but my reaction back then was simply that the next thing the poor young lady would surely want to do would be to rush off to wash her hands!

Another thing that surprises me is how people clam up whenever the subject of 'Relativity' is mentioned. This fascinating topic is a certain conversation-stopper in most situations, and definitely not a subject to be brought up on a first date (or on any date for that matter, as I've found out to my cost).

Einstein's Special Theory of Relativity deals with the measurements of time and distance by two people who are moving at a steady speed relative to each other, while his much more complicated General Relativity Theory deals with measurements where accelerations or gravitational fields are involved rather than just steady speeds. The core ideas in Einstein's Special Theory are really quite straightforward, but the maths in his General Theory is way beyond my grasp.

The main obstacle to getting to grips with his theories is that the consequences that they predict fly in the face of what we accept as 'common sense'. However, we often form ideas based on limited experience that turn out to be untrue when we apply them to new unfamiliar situations.

For example, it's easy to think that because objects we throw into the air always come back down again, that this will be the case however fast we throw them up. However, this is not true. If we could throw an object up faster than a critical speed, (the escape velocity of the Earth at sea level which is 7 miles per second), it would not come back down.

In a similar vein, we can accept the fact that a bird may fly past us at say 10 mph, an aeroplane may fly over us at 600 mph, and a satellite may pass overhead at 5 miles per second. It seems a reasonable guess that an object could travel past us at any speed, but this is not the case. There is a 'speed limit'. Light can only travel at this 'speed limit', and light is the only thing that can travel that fast. Solid objects can only travel past you at less than the 'speed limit'.

Whenever you discover a new fact about something, if it contradicts what you would have expected to be the case based on your experience of the world, you should also expect that as a consequence, other 'facts' you previously accepted as true may also turn out to be incorrect. That is precisely what Einstein did. The new fact in his case, which was established experimentally at the end of the 19th century, was that when the speed of light is measured, it always turns out to be the same fixed speed, regardless of the speed of the source of the light in relation to the person doing the measuring. Now on the face of it this all sounds harmless stuff, but Einstein's genius was to see that when you carefully consider the consequences of this new fact, many of our accepted 'common sense' ideas about time and space quickly fall apart. His Special Theory of Relativity is based on just two things:

1. *The reasonable assumption that nobody is in a 'special' position. The laws of nature are the same for everyone who is moving at a steady speed (i.e. not being pushed or pulled, nor influenced by a gravitational field).*
2. *The new fact, that two people moving at a steady speed relative to each other, will both measure the speed of a pulse of light to be the same fixed speed, regardless of the speed of the light source relative to them.*

If anyone were rash enough to ask me to explain the core ideas in Relativity, I would explain them as follows, but if the topic is really not your thing, skip on to Page 84. Imagine a situation where Fred and his partner Freda are jogging towards each other at a steady closing speed of 10 mph. Just as they pass each other, Fred throws a ball away from him at 30 mph in the direction he is travelling, which is towards his dog Fido. At the same instant Freda throws a ball away from her at 30 mph, the same speed as Fred did, but in the opposite direction to the one she is travelling in.

From Fred's point of view, his ball shoots off towards Fido, and Freda's ball follows it at a slower speed. His ball reaches Fido first. He can calculate the speed of Freda's ball relative to him as 20 mph by subtracting the 10 mph she is moving away from him at, from the 30 mph she threw her ball at.

From Freda's point of view, her ball shoots off towards Fido, and follows Fred's ball, but at a slower speed. Fred's ball reaches Fido first. She can calculate the speed of Fred's ball relative to her as 40 mph by adding the 10 mph he is moving away from her at, to the 30 mph he threw his ball at. So far, this all seems to be just 'common sense'.

Bearing Einstein's two starting ideas in mind, if instead of Fred and Freda each throwing a ball, they each hold a torch and flash a pulse of light from it towards Fido, an intriguing situation develops. From both Fred and Freda's points of view, because we are now dealing with light pulses, they will both measure that both pulses travel away from them at the same fixed speed and reach Fido together. For both Fred and Freda, the light pulses leaving the torches are the first event that occurs, and the pulses reaching Fido are the second event that occurs.

<u>Now for the key point</u>: Due to their relative motion, Fred and Freda will measure that the pair of light pulses travelled a different distance between leaving the torches and reaching Fido. However, as they both calculate the relative speed of the light pulses by dividing the distance they travelled by the time they took, and come up with the same fixed speed, as well as measuring a different <u>distance</u> between the two events, they must be measuring that a different <u>time</u> passed between the two events as well!

Fred, Freda and Fido - Scenario No. 1

In everyday life we are used to simply adding or subtracting two speeds to calculate a resulting speed. When somebody throws a ball away from them at a certain speed, if we want to calculate the speed of the ball from our own point of view, we add or subtract the speed that the person is moving relative to us to the speed that they threw the ball.

Fred and Freda approach each other at a closing speed of 10 mph.

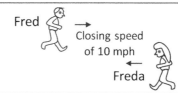

Just as they pass each other, they each propel a ball away from them to the right at a speed of 30 mph for their dog Fido to try to catch.

From Fred's point of view, his ball reaches Fido first. Freda's ball travels away from him at 20 mph because Freda was moving at a relative speed of 10 mph in the opposite direction to the ball she threw.

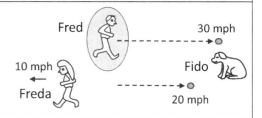

From Freda's point of view, Fred's ball reaches Fido first. Fred's ball travels away from her at 40 mph because Fred was moving at a relative speed of 10 mph in the same direction as the ball he threw.

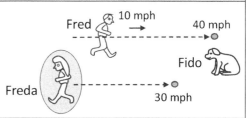

In the time it takes for Fred's ball to reach Fido, Fred measures that both of the balls move away from him less distance than Freda measures they move away from her. This is because they disagree about the speed of the balls. If Fred divides the distance his ball moved by the time it took, he calculates its speed to be 30 mph, and if he does the same for Freda's ball, he calculates 20 mph. If Freda divides the distance her ball moved by the time, she calculates its speed to be 30 mph, and if she does the same for Fred's ball, she calculates 40 mph.

Fred, Freda and Fido - Scenario No. 2

As in Scenario No. 1, the laws of physics work the same for Fred and Freda as they move at a constant speed relative to each other. However, a pulse of light behaves very differently to a ball. Both Fred and Freda will always measure the speed of the light pulses from both of their torches to be the same fixed speed of light, even though the other person's torch is moving relative to them.

Fred and Freda approach each other at a closing speed of 10 mph.

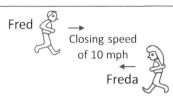

Just as they pass each other they each flash a pulse of light from their torch to the right, towards their dog Fido.

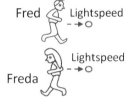

From Fred's point of view, both pulses travel at the same fixed speed of light, and a short time later both reach Fido. Meanwhile, Freda continues to move away towards the left.

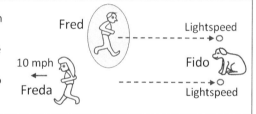

From Freda's point of view, both pulses travel at the same fixed speed of light, and a short time later both reach Fido. Meanwhile, Fred continues to move away towards the right.

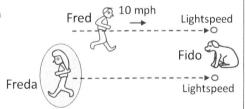

Now for the key point: Fred measures that the light pulses move away from him less distance than Freda measures they move away from her. However, because they are light pulses, when Fred and Freda measure their speed, they will come up with the same answer, and agree they are moving at the speed of light. As SPEED is calculated as the DISTANCE travelled divided by the TIME taken, it follows that Fred and Freda must be measuring the TIME the light took to reach Fido to be different as well as the DISTANCE it travelled.

The track meanders for about five miles until I reach a road into the village of Ogbourne St George. I turn right onto it and go up the hill to the village. Once there, I turn left, go under a main road and walk on through the village for a few hundred yards.

Having just established that Fred and Freda will measure the time passing between the same two events to be different, we can now go further with Special Theory. Let's imagine that Fred and Freda are each wearing a watch. What if the two events being considered happen to be two successive ticks of Fred's watch, or two successive ticks of Freda's watch? It turns out that for Fred, the time passing between the ticks of Freda's watch is longer than the time passing between the ticks of his own watch. Similarly, for Freda, the time passing between the ticks of Fred's watch is longer than the time passing between the ticks of her own watch. Life will go on normally for both of them, but they will both measure that the other person's watch, which is moving relative to them, is ticking at a slower rate than their own watch, which is not moving relative to them. This sounds crazy! How can they <u>both</u> measure that time is slowing down for the other person who is moving relative to them?

The explanation is that they will never agree that two events happening some distance apart actually happened simultaneously. As their relative motion causes them to measure the time that passes between two events to be different, if either of them happened to measure that 'no time' had passed between two particular events because the events occurred simultaneously, the other person will measure that 'some time' had passed. If either of them claim that two particular events occurred simultaneously, the other one will always disagree and claim that they are not comparing events that are simultaneous.

When Fred notes that his watch measures a certain time has passed since he passed Freda, he calculates that Freda's moving watch is <u>simultaneously</u> measuring less time. However, Freda will not agree that Fred is comparing the two watches simultaneously. When Freda notes that her watch measures a certain time has passed since she passed Fred, she calculates that Fred's moving watch is <u>simultaneously</u> measuring less time. However, Fred will not agree that Freda is comparing the two watches simultaneously. When they *both compare what their two watches simultaneously record, they are simply not comparing the same two 'watch events'. The greater the relative speed between Fred and Freda, the greater the slowing effect is. If it were possible for them to travel relative to each other at the speed of light, which it is not, they would each calculate that the other person's watch had slowed so much it had stopped ticking altogether!*

The effects of relative motion between two people include:

- *For both of them a moving watch ticks at a slower rate than one that is not moving relative to them.*
- *For both of them the length of a moving object is contracted in its direction of motion.*
- *They will not agree that two particular events some distance apart occurred simultaneously.*
- *If they sum any two relative speeds that are each less than the speed of light, the answer will not be the same as doing a simple addition of the two speeds and will always be less than the speed of light.*
- *If any speed is added to or subtracted from the speed of light, the answer will always be the speed of light.*
- *No object can travel relative to them at or faster than the speed of light (it is our universe's 'speed limit').*

So why don't we notice these effects in everyday life? Although the effects are present at all relative speeds, it is only at relative speeds that are a significant proportion of the speed of light that they become noticeable. As light travels at the phenomenal speed of three hundred thousand kilometres per second, at everyday speeds, even for passengers on planes travelling at six hundred kilometres per hour, the effects are there but they are minute.

This means it's quite safe for us to continue to simply add speeds when we are doing things like throwing a ball or flying in an aeroplane because the speeds involved are such a tiny fraction of the speed of light. The answers we get are not absolutely accurate, but they are fine for all practical purposes. However, this is not the case for scientists who are dealing with atomic particles moving at speeds close to the speed of light or engineers making extremely accurate GPS measurements. They have to make sure they take Einstein's theories fully into account in their calculations.

The road bends sharp right, and after a few yards I turn left into trees to start climbing the hill up to Barbury Castle. This section is called Smeathe's Ridge, and under normal circumstances would be a beautiful walk up the grassy turf with extensive views all around. However, this is not normal times. I feel shattered and soon find myself stopping every few minutes. I just stand still and bend over for literally twenty seconds, and then carry on again. As I bend over and catch sight of my bare legs, something seems to be rippling under my skin. I think it must be the blood pulsing around, but it looks rather like in those CGI horror films like 'The Mummy' where lots of little beetles are crawling about under the unfortunate victim's skin. Goodness knows what good stopping and bending over does, but I just keep doing it and it seems to help. However, it slows me right down. After what seems an eternity I reach the Barbury Castle checkpoint in a car park. A cheerful young couple with a small dog welcome me, and look after me really well. Even the dog makes a big fuss of me.

Barbury Castle checkpoint

Arrival time at checkpoint: Sunday 10:33

Stage distance: 10.5 miles
Time taken to complete the stage: 4:05
Average speed for the stage: 2.57 mph

Distance since starting: 79.9 miles
Time taken since starting: 24:29
Average speed since starting: 3.26 mph

Distance left to Avebury: 6.1 miles

79.9

0 miles   Distance since starting   86 miles

0 hours   Time taken since starting   28 hours

10: Barbury Castle to Avebury (6.1 miles)

My coffee cup is filled and I set off again. I walk through the massive hill fort, but can't see much of the layout. These sorts of features are shown to best advantage from a distance, or in this case from the air. The Ridgeway Path descends a bit and bears to the left. An elderly couple, even older and more doddery than me, get out of a large car and start walking along the path ahead of me. They are walking slowly, and he is limping slightly and has a walking stick. I follow them for some time, and to my dismay I find they are getting away from me! I must be going really slowly now. It's about five more miles to Avebury. Ahead of me is Hackpen Hill, which is my last obstacle. This is a beautiful place. For me, there is something special about clusters of pine trees. It is an ancient landscape, with Sarsen stones visible in the fields either side of me. I must keep a good look out for a signpost after about four miles which will direct me off the Ridgeway onto an ancient path called the Herepath which takes you into Avebury. The last thing I want to do at this late stage is to miss it and go the wrong way. I feel my mood lift and I start to feel optimistic about finishing within time. Surely I can walk these last few miles! My rucksack is feeling very uncomfortable now, so I remind myself to buy a new one. I think we still have a few books of Green Shield stamps somewhere at home. I wonder if they still take them?

I was sitting at home on my fiftieth birthday when, turning the TV on, I saw a lady using British Sign Language. I don't know quite why, but then and there I decided to try to learn to sign. I enrolled in local evening classes and really enjoyed it. The whole structure of the language is different to spoken languages. It soon became clear to me that I would not make any real progress unless I mixed with the Deaf, so I made some enquiries and was able to go along to a local Deaf Club. Going there was one of the most challenging things I have ever attempted. It was way out of my comfort zone, and I felt really helpless and exposed while I was there. However, they were very supportive, and I soon made a number of friends. I found it very hard to learn, but I persevered for around five years, and while I got quite good at signing what I wanted to say, I was nothing like as good at understanding what they were signing to me. I could understand if they made it direct and simple for me, but got lost when they signed with each other at their normal speed.

When I retired from the job I had been doing for over thirty years, I was completely unprepared for the feeling of immense relief that I felt for the first weeks after I left. I hadn't realised just how much of a mental strain I had been under during the preceding years, having to go into work day after day at the beck and call of other people, responding to their every whim. I had enjoyed many aspects of my work life, but now it was as if a heavy weight had suddenly been lifted from me. I decided I wanted to carry on doing some sort of work, but something quite different.

After some thought I decided to start working part time at the local Further Education College supporting a deaf student using my signing skills. However, when my student dropped out of college, as the college already had other support staff for deaf students, I was assigned instead to support students with a range of needs who needed help in the classroom.

I thoroughly enjoyed my seven years at the college, supporting students on many different courses. One young lady I supported in I.T. refused to talk out loud at all, but once she got to know me she was happy to whisper to me. She was obsessed with only two subjects: the Titanic and Harry Potter. When the tutor set the students a major project, allowing them to choose whatever subject interested them, she of course chose the Titanic. She thought I knew absolutely everything about everything, and asked me searching questions about the ship's layout which I doubt even its captain could have answered. For example, can you get directly up the stairs from 'E Deck' to the Ballroom? I always gave her a plausible answer, but I confess that I had to resort to bluffing some of the time.

Another student was a lad called Nigel who was a Goth, and the first thing he said to me when I met him was that he had been nocturnal for two years. His leather jacket was festooned in chains which all seemed to be attached to other chains. I got on well with Nigel, but what with the computer mouse, the keyboard and his various text books, as we worked together we kept getting tangled up in his chains.

My favourite activity was supporting in the small animals section. I used to help several students in the class with their handwriting. On one occasion, I happened to comment that there seemed to suddenly be a large number of baby rabbits in the rabbit run. The young ladies looked at me as if I was completely naïve, and gently explained to me that some weeks before, Sven had 'got out'. I said, "Who is Sven?" and they pointed to a large cage with an enormous grey rabbit in it who was staring hard at me. I put two and two together, and just said, "Oh, I see," and left it at that.

The students obviously wanted to broaden my education, and insisted that I had a go at feeding Malcolm. Malcolm turned out to be a rather large green snake. I was equipped with safety glasses, stout gauntlets and a pair of very long tweezers. They carefully slid the glass front of the snake box open a couple of inches and encouraged me to poke the tweezers in holding a small chunk of food. Nothing happened. Malcolm just stayed coiled up and completely motionless. "He's not hungry," I said. "No wait, he takes his time," they said. I sat there holding the tweezers. One by one the students in the class clustered round, until half of the class had joined me. They all stood behind me in silence staring intently at Malcolm. The minutes went by and my arm started to ache. Suddenly, and without warning, Malcolm struck. He snatched the food and, startled, we all jumped back two steps in unison. I nearly fell off the stool I was perched on. One young lady came over to me as I composed myself and said, helpfully but belatedly, "Malcolm always makes us jump."

I supported three students on Business I.T. courses. The tutor was a lovely Chinese lady called Mrs Lee. I am average height, but I towered over Mrs Lee. She had one difficult student who was well over six foot, whose behaviour was always causing problems in class. One day his father came in, and told Mrs Lee that if his son caused any trouble, she had his permission to beat him! The idea of the diminutive Mrs Lee even being able to reach up to the lad to beat him was completely ridiculous. You can't help wondering if the father was the source of the boy's behavioural problems.

On one occasion Mrs Lee did not seem to be her normal cheerful self, so I asked her if everything was alright. She said she had to go into hospital for an operation the following week. I dutifully said the things one normally says such as, "I'm sorry to hear that, I hope it's nothing serious." She came over to me and half covering her mouth so nobody else could hear, she stretched up to me and whispered in her strong Chinese accent, "Wimins pwoblems." Being a man, I immediately changed the subject, and being British, I changed it to talking about the weather outlook.

I was fortunate to be assigned to support a young man who had Muscular Dystrophy. He was a quadriplegic, and although he could talk and eat normally, his only movement was in his fingers which he used to operate his electric wheelchair. I supported him for three years on an Art and Design course, doing the manual things under his direction that he wasn't able to do. It was a good course, and he did well. When he left college, I continued our friendship by visiting him once a fortnight at his home for a couple of hours for a chat. He was an expert on Football and James Bond films, and I'm certain he would have aced Mastermind on either subject. In the twelve years I knew him I never once heard him complain or say a cross word to anybody. In spite of our great age difference, we both had the same sense of humour, and were able to make each other laugh. Sadly he died aged just thirty one. Life can be very unfair. He was one of the most courageous and determined people I have had the good fortune to know, and I miss him.

I can now see Avebury ahead of me further down the valley. What a welcome sight. A wave of relief comes over me. I am not feeling in such good physical shape now, and I have to constantly tell myself to keep moving. At last I see the signpost directing me into Avebury. I turn off the Ridgeway Path with one mile to go.

When I started out as a young man designing computer systems for clients I was very 'green' and lacking in confidence. On my first big customer project, I was part of a team of five. A series of business meetings had been set up over a period of several days in a swanky hotel near Croydon where our team could work alongside the client's team. I was not used to hotels or dining out, and I hardly drank alcohol, so I felt very apprehensive about the whole affair. I arrived at the hotel on the first evening and booked into my room. Even that had been an ordeal. We all sat down to dinner at a large round table which seated about a dozen people. I nervously did my best to make intelligent conversation with the high-powered clients either side of me. When a waiter came around to take orders, I grabbed a menu and was dismayed to see it was all written in French. I made a stab at looking as if I was reading it and pointed at one of the main courses. The waiter took my menu, did a sort of small bow and disappeared. Time went by, and I tried not to drink too much of the wine, although everyone else was really knocking it back. It was only when waiters started arriving with the first of the ordered meals that it struck me like a thunderbolt that I didn't know what I had ordered!

How would I know which of the meals being proffered to us to claim as mine. I had several close calls when nobody appeared to be claiming a meal, and assumed it must be mine, but just in time somebody turned from their animated conversation and claimed it. I died a thousand deaths that evening. Fortunately, a waiter came straight towards me and placed a meal down in front of me. I think he was probably the one who took my order, but it was hard to tell because they all looked alike to me, dressed in their penguin outfits and wearing their superior expressions. The waiter then offered me a baffling range of things I could sprinkle on my meal, all of which I declined to keep life as simple as possible. I had learned one important lesson: It never pays to bluff because it can come back to bite you!

Although I enjoy the odd drink, and I enjoy chatting with a few friends, I am not comfortable when thrust into large social gatherings. At work I was not always able to avoid them, and I was particularly like a fish out of water when obliged to attend the frequent 'compulsory enjoyment' social events which certain of my colleagues engineered. When we arrived at a venue, the instigator of the event would rush to the bar to order a round of drinks for everybody, and while the bartender was sorting out his order, he would swiftly down two or three 'shorts' to kickstart his alcohol level. (We referred to such shorts as 'lurkers'). I suppose the extra drinks must have been necessary for him to function properly and become the 'life and soul of the party'. The capacity of those guys was way out of my league. In the end I only got through such sessions by adopting what I think of as my 'G&T trick'. I started with a gin and tonic, which I *nursed, and in subsequent rounds, I simply topped up my half-full glass with plain tonic water. That way I always appeared to have a drink in my hand, which was in fact getting weaker and weaker as the evening wore on.*

Suddenly, I realise that the person standing by the side of the track a few yards ahead of me is my long-suffering wife. I have to admit that an eighty six mile event is not a spectator sport, and I am grateful for the support she always gives me. In my dreamlike state, I have forgotten that I have already turned off the Ridgeway, and assume she has walked much further out of the village to meet me than she actually has. She can't understand why I keep insisting that we must look out for a right turn into Avebury. It is only when we walk into the outskirts of the village that I wake up to where I am, and acknowledge that she is right and I am wrong. I get my first glimpse of the famous stone circle, thought to date back to before 2000 BC.

Given my character, which people generally seem to see as quiet and introverted, it came as a considerable surprise to me when I discovered that I had a real talent for speaking in public and making audiences laugh. It started at work, where I had to create and then deliver business presentations and software product demonstrations. Over the years, I delivered them to clients who were more and more senior, and to larger and larger audiences.

As if that wasn't a big enough surprise, they morphed into 'after-dinner speaking' spots at my company's Branch Meetings. This gave me the opportunity to poke fun at senior management, which went down well with the audience, and also gave me the satisfaction of striking a few blows in my private anti-authority campaign. My humour owed more to my hero Les Dawson than anyone else. My delivery and timing were spot on, and it helped considerably that I was usually the only one in the room who hadn't been drinking. For me, entertaining audiences of over one hundred people was both risky and scary, but tremendously intoxicating and addictive. It acted on me like a drug, and I revelled in the applause. I felt that I held the audience in the palm of my hand. It was like being on a surfboard riding a giant wave. As the audience laughed and my adrenalin surged, I had to rein back my euphoric reaction and concentrate on keeping to my rehearsed patter. I had to work hard to keep myself balanced on the crest of that wave. (I should point out that I have never actually been on a surfboard, let alone ridden a giant wave.) When my 'performance' was over, I felt completely drained for quite some time. After one well-received speech, a salesman I worked with gave me a puzzled look and said, "You know, when you go up there you become a completely different person." Of course, I wasn't a different person, he was just seeing a side of me that I suppress in all other situations in life.

It was like riding a giant wave.

I knew that when I was up there holding the microphone, I had permission to 'act out a role' where different rules from normal life applied. I was 'in control', but the moment I handed the microphone back I would completely relinquish the power I had been given. How much my confidence had grown compared to how I felt at that first business meal in the hotel, and in just thirty short years!

Seeing the finish banner just ahead, I break into a shuffling jog, which leaves my wife some distance behind me. She dashes off another quick snap of me for the album. (When we looked at the photo later, although I do appear in it in the distance, there is a charming closeup of a family of smiling Chinese tourists and a local cat). As I progress down Avebury high street, weaving a little from side to side, I distinctly hear a small child sitting in her buggy say to her mother, "Why is that man running so slowly?" The child's mother diplomatically replies, "Shh... I'm sure he is doing his best dear." I resist the urge to go over to the child and say, "Now look here sunshine, how fast would you be running after eighty six miles?" Ahead are a small group of people who applaud as I touch the banner marking the finish line. I make the most of my few brief seconds in the limelight by casually waving in the manner of royalty to acknowledge their applause. I brace myself for the inevitable rush of autograph hunters, but only one person comes up to me. "Well, at least I've got one fan!" I think to myself. "Just after your tracker mate!" he says, as he removes the tracking device taped to my rucksack. In an instant, the mental pressure I have been inflicting on myself to relentlessly keep plodding on evaporates, and I feel nothing but elation. Only I know what I have been through, and although there are people all around me, I feel utterly alone. For almost twenty seven hours I have not been able to relax, constantly aware that time was ticking by. I will borrow the words of the poet Andrew Marvell to convey how this made me feel, because his words are much more eloquent than mine could ever be: 'but at my back I always hear, time's winged chariot hurrying near'.

Avebury checkpoint

Arrival time at checkpoint: Sunday 12:58

Stage distance: 6.1 miles
Time taken to complete the stage: 2:25
Average speed for the stage: 2.52 mph

Distance since starting: 86.0 miles
Time taken since starting: 26:54
Average speed since starting: 3.20 mph

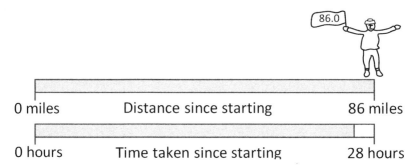

0 miles	Distance since starting	86 miles

| 0 hours | Time taken since starting | 28 hours |

Permission to stop and permission to carry on

For hours I had refused to even entertain the thought of stopping and taking a rest. To spur me on, the rather pathetic mantra that I repeated over and over again in my head had been, "If you don't keep going you won't get there!" As I touched the finish banner a wave of relief swept over me, and I consciously told myself, "It's alright, you have my 'permission' to stop now."

At the finish, I was presented with a large medal, and asked if I wanted to see any of the medical staff who were on hand. I thanked them, but declined, having had a scare years earlier on the Snowdonia Marathon when I almost fell into the hands of a group of keen Welsh St John's Ambulance ladies. Four or five of them were lined up by the roadside at the twenty mile mark. I could see that they were each holding various bits of medical equipment, some of which had ominous 'invasive' looking tubes and clips attached. As I staggered past them, I speculated that they had just taken delivery of some new equipment which they were dying to try out on a fallen runner, preferably a man. I remember quickening my pace until they were well out of sight.

On a previous occasion, I made the mistake of going into the hall at the finish and sitting down for half an hour with my wife for a cup of tea. Although this revived me, my muscles all stiffened up, and my legs became fixed rigid in 'sitting in a chair' shape. My poor wife had to help me, as I hobbled bent over to our car a few hundred yards away. I must have looked as if I was sitting in a wheelchair, but without the wheelchair. As she supported me, she constantly whispered words of encouragement in my ear such as, "I told you this would happen! You never listen to me! Why can't you just do the things normal men do at your age, like take up golf?" This time, I stayed on my feet and kept on the move for half an hour or more before I walked to the car park with my wife, where I had a cup of coffee and a bite to eat. Thankfully, my feet were in good shape, and it was a miracle that I had no blisters! At the end of the event, all I can say is, compared to a normal routine weekend, "What a fantastic adventure it had been!"

My wife, who had been concerned about me attempting the event in the first place, was relieved at my safe arrival. She said, as she always does after an event, "Well, now you've done it and got it out of your system, you can call it a day. Why not just do half marathons from now on?" This immediately posed the problem for me of how I was going to persuade her to give me 'permission' to carry on and have another go at the Ridgeway Challenge the following year?

Later, after some thought, I realised that to get around the problem some emotional blackmail was called for. I came up with a cunning plan, so cunning that even Baldrick would be proud of it. In front of our friends I told her that although I have completed the challenge twice so far and have two medals to show for it, I would dearly like to do it just one more time to get a third medal. That would mean that I could then leave a medal to each of our three children for them to remember me by when I am no longer around. My friends' reaction was to say to her, "Oh what a lovely thought. You know, you are so lucky to have such a thoughtful and considerate husband." In reply, my wife just forced a smile and, through gritted teeth, said "Yes I am, aren't I."

Only one runner finished behind me, but during the event around forty runners had retired at various checkpoints along the way. If you pull out in the first half of the route you are transported to Checkpoint 5, and if you pull out in the second half you are transported to Avebury, so runners are always looked after and nobody is ever left stuck out in the wilds.

An examination of my times at each checkpoint shows that my speed steadily declined throughout the event, and my overall average was 3.2 mph. The leading runners' average speed was around 7 mph, which is faster than I can run flat out when I am fresh! At the start of any event, you only have a certain store of energy to expend, depending on how well you have prepared yourself by proper training and the right diet. During an event you can choose how to expend your energy reserve. You could be cautious and use it up by going at a deliberately slower pace, but then you run the risk of running out of time, or even having energy left at the finish. The other extreme is to start off fast and risk running out of steam part way through a long event.

In events up to a marathon distance of twenty six miles, I don't find it too difficult to pace myself. However, in an eighty six mile endurance event like the Ridgeway Challenge, I find it extremely hard to judge the right pace for the first twenty or so miles. I don't want to go too quickly in the early stages, spurred on by adrenalin and excitement, only to conk out before the half way point. I simply press on with a sense of urgency right from the start because I am aware that each checkpoint has a cut-off time, and I must beat them all if I am to qualify as a finisher. Starting in the earlier group means I have two hours extra time, so it is only the checkpoints towards the end of the event that cause me any real concern. In my case, the concept of taking things too slowly and having any spare energy left at Avebury is frankly ridiculous!

Checkpoint number	1	2	3	4	5	6	7	8	9	10
Distance from start in miles	10.5	16.8	26.2	34.2	41.7	52.4	61.5	69.4	79.9	86
Average speed for 24 hours	3.59	3.59	3.59	3.59	3.59	3.59	3.59	3.59	3.59	3.59
Actual average stage speed	4.25	3.75	3.59	3.43	3.30	3.06	3.08	3.06	2.57	2.52
Actual average speed so far	4.25	4.05	3.87	3.76	3.67	3.52	3.45	3.40	3.26	3.20

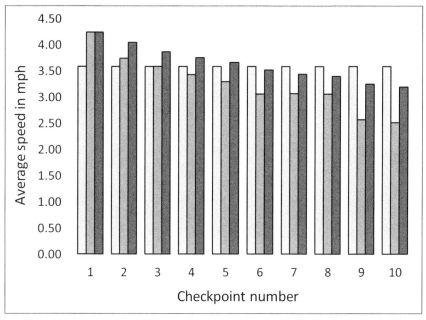

In the chart, the light grey bars represent a speed of 3.59 mph, which is the speed I would have to average for the whole event to do it in under twenty four hours.

The middle bars show my actual average speed between each of the checkpoints. These start off strongly, but drop off at each subsequent checkpoint.

The darker bars show my overall average speed from the start of the event as I arrive at each of the checkpoints.

The solid line on this chart shows the actual time I took to get to each of the ten checkpoints. The dotted line shows the times I should have reached each checkpoint by if I was maintaining an average speed of 3.59 mph throughout the event, which would have meant I would finish in just under 24 hours.

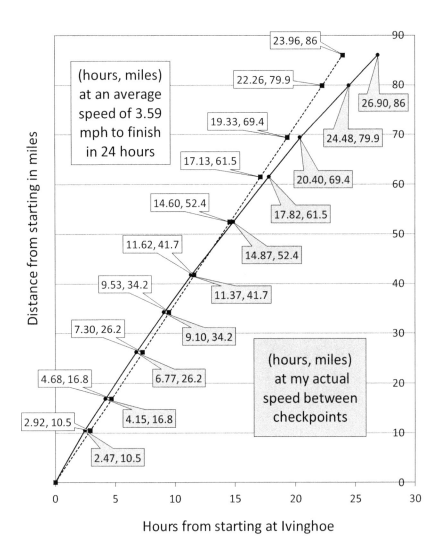

Hours from starting at Ivinghoe

At South Stoke Checkpoint 5, which is almost half way, I am still slightly ahead of time, but my time slips more and more at the later checkpoints, particularly the last two.

Throughout the event, my mental and physical state were constantly changing. This 'unscientific' chart illustrates how my appetite, my assessment of my physical shape, the mental effort I was making, and my mood fluctuated as time went by.

The food I ate gradually tasted less and less palatable during the first half, and when I arrived at South Stoke, the smell of food being cooked instantly turned my stomach. For the rest of the event, I was only able to tolerate sweet tea or coffee and bananas. However, within an hour of finishing I started to fancy food again.

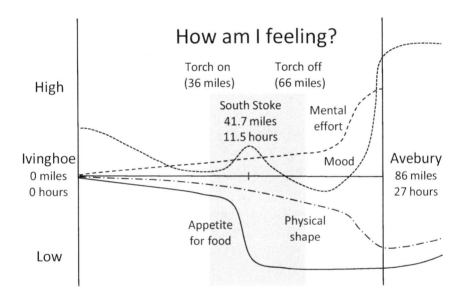

Right up to the Sparsholt Firs checkpoint I felt in good physical shape, although tired. After that I felt it declined, declining much more steeply during the last sixteen miles after the Foxhill checkpoint. Within an hour of finishing, by keeping on the move, I was in tolerable shape, still able to walk and not feeling too stiff.

At the start, my mood was positive and I felt on a real high because of the adrenalin. This gradually wore off, but picked up again as I neared the halfway point at South Stoke. After that it declined and I felt low for most of the way to Barbury Castle. My mood then picked up as I began the last six miles to Avebury, and for the last half mile after meeting my wife, I felt elated. The feeling of elation persisted for quite some time after the event.

The mental effort needed to force myself to keep pressing on increased gradually all the way to Foxhill. From there on, it rapidly ramped right up, and was really intense during my climb up to Barbury Castle. At the finish line, I was simply able to 'let go', and the mental pressure I was feeling instantly dropped to zero.

After Checkpoint 6, to have any chance of finishing in under twenty four hours, I needed to lift my average speed for the rest of the event above 3.59 mph. Clearly, I didn't manage to do this, and my average speed from the start was gradually pulled lower and lower. After Checkpoint 8, my average speed really dropped off a cliff as I was getting very tired both physically and mentally.

Following the event, having gathered my wits and prepared a polished and convincing description of my heroic performance, the next problem I faced was how I could encourage my friends to ask me how I had got on, without them realising that I was prompting them to do so.

The reason I adopt this highly regrettable but necessary tactic is that, although my parents gave me a good upbringing, as a child I was taught to see any form of 'showing off' as a bad thing. Unfortunately, being branded a 'show off' was a sure way to quickly extinguish any display of individuality or free spirit in me. I can still hear my parents saying, "You know it's not good to blow your own trumpet." Inevitably, I turned out to be one of those introverted souls destined to grow up in life without a trumpet. I try not to drop remarks into conversations that are too obvious such as, "Did you know I went on a long walk last weekend?" No, my approach is much more subtle than that. To start with I might casually ask, "Have you seen what the National Trust are doing in Avebury?" They are likely to answer, "No, what are they doing?" and then I am off, like a rat up a drainpipe. However, because 'knowing my place' and 'not pushing myself forward' is so ingrained in me from childhood, when anybody swallows the bait and does heap the praise on me that I have been seeking, I rebuff it and insist that it was nothing, I didn't do that well, and I make light of it all. This whole charade which I act out is a source of intense frustration for my poor wife whose reaction is, "Why don't you just wear your Ridgeway Challenge T-shirt the whole time?" What complicated creatures we humans are, or maybe it is just me! I asked my daughter, who is a Clinical Psychologist, if the material in this book would make a good case study, and she assured me that there is enough here for a whole conference.

A candid self-assessment

I have assessed my performance on each of thirty personal challenges. Some are outdoor activities, and others are attempts to acquire a new skill. When my wife looked at my list she was surprised that I had not put 'staying married for fifty odd years' at the top of it, as she would have done. I assured her that being married to her had been a privilege and a joy rather than a challenge, which rendered her speechless, at least for a while.

I hesitated before including the next paragraph because I was concerned I would sound like an amateur psychologist spouting nonsense. I asked my wife for her opinion, and she said I should definitely include it, adding "Why break the habits of a lifetime?"

I suspect that my expectations of what I would achieve in adult life were heavily influenced by the fictitious heroes I was exposed to as I grew up. I remember reading about Dan Dare's exploits in comics, seeing Flash Gordon at Saturday morning pictures, and following the daring adventures of tough commandoes in war films as they raided the enemy coast. The characters involved were all able to effortlessly climb overhanging cliffs, abseil into deep ravines, and expertly pilot all manner of planes, boats and rockets. Unfortunately, these adventures lived only in my vivid imagination, not in real life. As a result, when I was older and I came to try my hand at various activities, I discovered that, while I shared their 'swashbuckling' enthusiasm, I was a lot more cautious and a lot less able than either Dan Dare or Flash Gordon. In adult life, I have had to accept the fact that I've failed to live up to my childhood image of myself as some sort of 'superman'.

I have asked myself these questions about each challenge:

- Did it stretch me and move me out of my comfort zone?
- How well do I feel I performed? Could I have done better?
- How enjoyable was it at the time and did I get a sense of achievement out of it afterwards?

The mark out of ten I have awarded myself indicates how well I feel I performed overall on each one:

- 1 out of 10 indicates a poor performance
- 5 out of 10 indicates an average performance
- 10 out of 10 indicates an excellent performance

3 out of 10 - Learning to swim

As a young teenager, learning to swim with my friends was very important to me at the time, and I think it stretched me a lot. When my games tutor thought I was ready, I remember the act of holding my breath and launching myself from the rail at the side of the pool to try to swim my first 'width'. I certainly felt a tremendous sense of achievement afterwards. However, I never did learn to breathe properly with my face in the water when doing the crawl, and I am not a strong swimmer. I did try, but never mastered, diving or jumping from the boards.

5 out of 10 - Duke of Edinburgh Award Scheme

Even though I was woefully unprepared for the conditions and poorly equipped, and had no previous experience of mountain walking, the expedition really did me a lot of good. It kickstarted a lifelong love of walking in the mountains. At fifteen, I suppose I must have had at least some 'drive' because I went back the following year to do the Silver Award.

2 out of 10 - Demonstrating leadership qualities

When my early attempts to assume leadership roles fizzled out, I remember deciding that this was not going to be my thing. I simply stopped trying to be a leader, and even declined opportunities when they presented themselves. However, I have always been interested in the process of leading, and over the years I have had the chance to closely observe other people successfully performing the role. I have tried to work out what it was that they were doing right, and why some were so much more successful than others. The successful ones were seen by people to be competent in the role, and had the ability to communicate a clear 'vision' to other people.

4 out of 10 – Learning to pilot a Glider

I think I was far too tense and nervous to get the most out of the gliding course. However, it certainly moved me out of my comfort zone, and I did feel a sense of achievement that I had at least managed to take-off, perform gentle manoeuvres and land successfully. My performance as a budding pilot turned out to be way below my dreams as a teenager.

8 out of 10 – Learning to pilot a Paraglider

I really enjoyed this experience, and I felt I made good progress in just two days. Some of the others on the course never did get airborne. It did stretch me and I am pleased that I really gave it a go and threw myself into it. It is something that I would like to have another go at.

1 out of 10 – Navigating in a car rally

My performance as a navigator was abysmal. I completely failed to foresee the inevitable problems I would encounter. I can't think why I agreed to do it and put myself in that position! It has given me great respect for the navigators in major car rallies who you see on TV sitting strapped in, and being bounced about in their seats as the driver flings the car around corners. They have to split their attention between glancing at the road and studying a map. How they manage to keep their last meal down I will never know!

7 out of 10 - Running marathons

I have always been well disciplined at preparing for long distance events, and I trained throughout the whole year in preparation for the Snowdonia Marathon that I ran in October each year. You always have to push yourself to complete a marathon distance, and so much can happen over a distance of twenty six miles. You can never a guarantee that you will finish. However, I was always a bit disappointed with my times which I didn't seem to be able to improve over the years. After each marathon, I always felt that I should have pushed myself a bit harder, especially for the last five miles.

6 out of 10 – Completing the Welsh 3000s

The Welsh 3000s is a really stretching event that I have yet to complete non-stop. It is a route that links several of my favourite walks in Wales. I have made a number of attempts at it on my own, trying a number of different approaches. I have given up trying to do it without support, and will try again with an outdoor adventure company that specialises in providing a complete 'support package' for clients. I am optimistic that I will manage to complete it at long last.

5 out of 10 – Learning to Tap Dance

I am not a natural dancer, and learning Tap Dancing has stretched me a lot. I really enjoy it and get a sense of achievement out of mastering the numerous steps. However, I had hoped I would be better at it by now. My main difficulty is speeding up the steps. I can learn them and do them at a steady pace, but when the pace really speeds up, I just can't make my feet tap quickly enough.

4 out of 10 – Learning to ride a Horse

As an adult, this is a difficult skill to master. I was certainly proud of myself for being able to do the basics of walking and trotting. I don't feel I am a very competent rider though. I have been unable to convince many of the horses I have ridden that I am the one in charge!

8 out of 10 - Building Woody the Wooden Horse

This was a worthwhile, but difficult, project to work on, which required a sustained effort over a period of several months. The end result exceeded my expectations. I enjoyed working on it immensely and got a sense of satisfaction afterwards, especially when I saw how much Woody was being used.

8 out of 10 - Walking around Jersey's coastal path

This is a great 48 mile walk which I always enjoy doing. It never feels anything like that far because of the beautiful scenery. There is something special about cliff paths. It's not a very risky enterprise though, because I can always get a bus back to St Aubin's Harbour if I have any problems!

3 out of 10 - Driving a Formula Ford at Goodwood

I am definitely not cut out to be a fast driver. I am the last person you would choose as the getaway driver if you were planning a bank robbery. Even if I could be taught to drive a car at racing speeds, I would never become a top driver because I have too much mechanical sympathy. I would always be trying to look after the engine and mechanics. In fact, I would be the exact opposite of the 'Top Gear' team!

4 out of 10 – Learning to paddle a Kayak

I was comfortable just paddling about, and felt quite confident. However, I was disappointed that I could not master righting a capsized kayak while I was still in it. This made progressing onto really rough water difficult because I was likely to turn it upside down frequently. Frustratingly, I just had to bale out and hang on to both paddle and kayak every time I capsized.

5 out of 10 – Learning Rock Climbing basics

I was in my forties when I first climbed a rockface, and it really stretched me because I had previously been scared of heights. I was not as good at it as I had hoped I would be, but I am quite proud of what I can do, and confident at scrambling.

7 out of 10 – Scrambling on the Cuillin Ridge

This was by far the most serious walking and scrambling I have undertaken. I got a great deal of satisfaction from my outings there. I had hoped to complete more peaks on the ridge, but my cautious approach limited what I attempted.

9 out of 10 - Climbing the Inaccessible Pinnacle

This was way out of my comfort zone, and I got a great sense of achievement from climbing it. I would have got even more out of it if I had been the lead climber!

8 out of 10 – Archery

As a complete novice, I found this easy, and did well. However, I am not comparing myself to somebody who does the sport seriously. I'm sure that experts have the target a lot further away than my targets were.

8 out of 10 - Clay Pigeon shooting

I was very surprised at how well I could shoot. The violent recoil of the gun takes some getting used to, but I was much better than I had expected to be. Again, I'm sure that it is made harder for those who take the sport seriously. I imagine that their clay pigeons are moving much faster than mine were.

3 out of 10 – Learning to sail a Dingy

I found it difficult to teach myself from a book, and was chuffed when I managed to perform all of the basic manoeuvres. As a child, I never had experience of any water-based activities. However, I never progressed beyond the basics, and was happy to just potter around for fun in a relaxed manner.

8 out of 10 - Ben Nevis circular walk

What a great walk in the snow this was! It really moved me on and made me feel confident that I could tackle some more ambitious walks. I had a great sense of achievement afterwards.

6 out of 10 - Running up Ben Nevis

A most memorable adventure! I realise now that I took a gamble and I was lucky to get away with it. I did at least prepare beforehand by researching the route and taking extra clothing with me. However, I underestimated the severity of the weather at the summit and how quickly it can change.

8 out of 10 - Aonach Eagach ridge in Glen Coe

I was very apprehensive when I first attempted this ridge after reading all sorts of dire warnings in climbing books about how difficult it was. I made sure that I took great care when I attempted it alone and felt elated when I managed it. The knife edge was challenging! It was another great memory.

7 out of 10 - Bidean Nam Bian in Glen Coe

It was a misty day for this walk, and once high up on the slopes in the cloud I felt very cut off from the rest of the world. I was disappointed that I could not see the views from the top, but crossing 'The Lost Valley' was an unforgettable experience.

3 out of 10 - Climbing Curved Ridge in Glen Coe

I just about got to the base of Curved Ridge and then turned back because of the rain. Disappointing, but I'm happy that I made the right decision under the circumstances.

8 out of 10 - Basics of Circular and Elliptical orbits

I found this an interesting mental challenge when I was young. It's easy to learn things when you are just spoon-fed them, but much more interesting and rewarding if you can work them out for yourself from first principles. I have always enjoyed building up my own mental picture of how things work.

9 out of 10 – Basics of Einstein's Special Theory

It's common knowledge what Einstein's two starting assumptions were, and the strange effects that they led to. What I find really interesting is explaining logically to myself step by step how his starting assumptions actually lead to the effects. I have derived immense satisfaction from working this out. It has been my greatest intellectual challenge.

7 out of 10 - Learning British Sign Language

At many levels, this was one of the hardest things I have ever tried to do. Going to Deaf Clubs in the early days pushed me way out of my comfort zone. I suppose I felt a bit like the Deaf must feel in the 'hearing' world. I was disappointed that in spite of making a great effort over a period of five years, although my signing became quite good, my receptive skill lagged behind. I got a great deal from the experiences I had with the Deaf, but I wish I could have put my hard-won skill to more practical use.

8 out of 10 - Supporting students at FE College

I feel I made a good job of supporting students, and for several of them I was able to significantly improve their college experience. The work was very satisfying, and I learnt a lot by being in the classroom for such a wide range of subjects.

9 out of 10 - Public Speaking

This was very stretching but also very rewarding. For me, it was the ultimate in 'risk-taking behaviour', bordering on 'reckless behaviour'. In the case of after-dinner speaking, to this day I am honestly not sure what it was that I was doing that made people laugh so much. I look back on my performances with many a chuckle and with a sense of pride.

Fortunately, history's heroes weren't like me

I would never claim that the world would be a better place if everybody was like me. In business, sport and generally in life, competitive people and people who are less cautious than I am get enjoyment from competing, innovating and exploring. Their boundless drive and energy are often what make important things happen in the world. Although I am happy as I am, I freely admit that historical events would have turned out very differently if the famous 'achievers' in history had had my cautious nature and my attitude to life:

Sir Edmund Hilary

When Hilary and Tenzing approached the foot of the Hilary Step near the summit of Everest, if I had been Hilary I might well have said, "You know Tenzing, I think we've done really well to get this high and I've really enjoyed it so far, but it's getting chilly, and this last bit looks a bit tricky. Let's go back down and have another go next year."

Neil Armstrong

When Armstrong and Aldrin had got close to the surface of the Moon, if I had been Armstrong I might have said, "Gee Buzz, great trip, really enjoyed it so far. There's only 30 seconds of fuel left, so let's abort. No point in taking any risks."

Lord Horatio Nelson

At a crucial point in the Battle of Trafalgar, if I had been Nelson I might have said, "Ok Hardy, terrific battle so far, but let's call it a day. I've already lost an eye and an arm so let's go home before I lose anything else and you start kissing me."

The Duke of Wellington

On the eve of the Battle of Waterloo, if I had been Wellington I might have said, "I've really enjoyed our march through some of the prettiest regions of France, but the men are tired. Tell them to pack away their weapons and take tomorrow off while we wait to see if the Prussians turn up."

Unfinished business and fresh adventures

There is an obvious problem with telling yourself, as I sometimes do, "Oh well, I can always try again next year." The problem is that, for all sorts of reasons, you don't always get another opportunity. One of my aunt's frequent sayings that I used to find chilling as a child was, "Enjoy yourself, it's later than you think!" When she said it I always shuddered, and imagined I could hear the distant slow chime of a single church bell.

With most things in life, you never know when you are doing them for the last time. For me, looking back on my adventures, I feel there are still many items of 'unfinished business'. There are also new challenges that I would like to have a go at. I am hoping to stay fit long enough to attempt at least some of them:

- Complete the Welsh 3000s non-stop 'in style'
- Complete the Welsh 3000s in under 20 hours
- Complete the Ridgeway Challenge for a third time
- Complete the Ridgeway Challenge in under 25 hours
  (Just possible if everything goes perfectly)
- Complete the Ridgeway Challenge when I am 80 years old
  (PDTMW)
- Complete the London Marathon once
  (If only I can just get a place!)
- Complete a 100 mile endurance event
  (PDTMW)
- Return to Curved Ridge in Glen Coe and climb it
- Explore more peaks in the Cuillin Ridge on Skye
- Drive an old Ford Popular just one more time

However, I have left it too late to tackle some challenges that I wanted to attempt earlier in my life, such as:

- Walking the whole length of the Cuillin Ridge (bypassing where possible those peaks requiring climbing skills)
- Learning the correct use of Crampons and Ice Axes
- Climbing Mont Blanc

(PDTMW : Please don't tell my wife)

Judging my ability and assessing the risks

I am not a competitive person, so I am not particularly concerned about my performance in relation to the performance of other people. As a rule of thumb, in marathons and endurance events, I fully accept that my times are always going to be two to three times longer than the times of the winners.

I often find it difficult to decide whether I am being too cautious, or just being sensible. Deciding what I think about a particular situation depends on the outcome of inner battles in my head between the 'safe and secure' side of me and the 'spartan and adventurous' side of me.

For example, when reflecting on what that child's mother said near the finish of the Ridgeway Challenge, did I really do my best? 'Safe and secure me' says, "Well done, you were just being sensible. You paced the eighty six miles very well, and at least you completed the distance. No point in pushing yourself too hard at your age!" However, 'spartan and adventurous me' says, "Come off it you wimp, surely you're not satisfied with that performance. You know in your heart that you can do better than that!"

I frequently muddy the water for myself by having several, sometimes vague, personal objectives for an event. In a marathon, for example, I may think to myself, "I want to complete the whole distance, but really I would like to do it in less than five hours, and I hope I can keep running the whole way." There are three distinct objectives there. Let's face it, no Olympic contender would think that way, they would simply be focused on winning.

I know that some folk have to battle constantly with poor health or family tragedies, and others face many challenges in life, but in this book I am only considering personal challenges I have chosen to tackle. I do realise that I am fortunate to be in such a position.

First, a couple of dictionary definitions:

- A challenge – to take part in a contest
- An adventure – a risky undertaking of unknown outcome

For me, a personal challenge is simply a contest with myself with a specific objective to aim for.

For me, an adventure is the process involved when I attempt to achieve a personal challenge that I have taken on. I accept that it will involve pushing the boundaries I normally set for myself and taking risks, and that it will stretch my physical and mental capabilities. When deciding whether to take on a particular challenge, my main concerns are:

- Do I want to do it, and would I be proud of myself if I did?
- Do I believe I am really capable of it?
- Just how risky is it? Are the risks acceptable?

This grid is an attempt to illustrate how I visualise personal challenges:

		NOT PHYSICALLY UP TO IT	NOT MENTALLY UP TO IT	RECKLESS BEHAVIOUR
	NO well beyond my ability	10 lengths in a swimming pool	Diving off the top board	Swimming the Channel
AM I CAPABLE OF IT?	YES but it will be a real stretch	AN ADVENTURE WITH LOW RISK Running a marathon	AN ADVENTURE WITH ACCEPTABLE RISK Crossing Crib Goch in the summer	RECKLESS BEHAVIOUR Aonach Eagach in a high wind
	YES well within my ability	ROUTINE WITH LOW RISK Going for a walk in the park	ROUTINE WITH ACCEPTABLE RISK Driving by car to Skye	RECKLESS BEHAVIOUR Riding a motorbike down the M1
		Risk is low	Risk is acceptable	Risk is too high

HOW RISKY IS IT?

We are all unique, with different abilities and different attitudes to risk. As a result, there is no 'correct' box in the grid to put a particular challenge, and you may feel the challenges belong in different places in the grid from me.

A straightforward routine task for one person may be a major challenge for somebody else. For example, somebody who has a phobia about going outdoors might place 'a walk in the park' in

109

the opposite corner of the grid. They may judge it to be far beyond their capability, and far too risky to contemplate. On the other hand, a competent endurance swimmer might see swimming the channel with the proper support as an 'adventure with acceptable risk' that they are quite capable of achieving.

Other factors can affect where you would put challenges in the grid. The act of attempting a challenge may change your ideas about where you would place a similar challenge in the future.

For example, some might see Crib Goch as an 'adventure with acceptable risk', as I do. However, after attempting it and completing it without encountering any problems, they may change its position in the grid to an 'adventure with low risk'. Alternatively, they may change it to 'reckless with high risk' if they had a bad experience, and swear they will never attempt it again.

You may also change where you position a challenge in the grid if you take steps to minimise or mitigate some of the risks that are concerning you. These are the sorts of things I have done at various times over the years to reduce risks to what I feel is an acceptable level:

- Spending time doing research and thorough preparation before attempting a challenge to determine the best route to follow, the terrain I will encounter, and the level of difficulty I will face.
- Going on a training course to gain knowledge and to learn new skills.
- Undertaking a training programme to improve my stamina and general level of fitness.
- Attending a course to improve my first aid skills.
- Going on a course to improve my level of confidence.
- Teaming up with other people who have some relevant experience.
- Hiring a qualified guide to accompany me.
- Employing the services of a company who can offer a full 'support package' that provides transport to the start and at the end of the challenge, a professional guide who knows the route and the terrain and has expertise in scrambling and first aid.
- Carrying a mobile phone, a torch, a whistle, a map, a compass, a survival bag and extra warm clothing, and leaving details of my planned route with somebody.

Did I succeed, fail or almost achieve?

My initial reaction to the prospect of a new challenge is usually enthusiasm:

- Cor, I'd really like to have a crack at doing that!
- Wouldn't it be fantastic if I could do it!
- Do I dare to have a go? Yes, I'll have a shot at it!

My enthusiasm often makes me over-optimistic about how well I will be able to perform the challenge. On the other hand, if I wasn't so optimistic, I probably wouldn't take some of them on in the first place. When it comes to actually doing it, my cautious nature means that although I am prepared to push myself, I am not prepared to push myself too far. With hindsight, I sometimes feel I have been too risk-averse, and allowed my caution to inhibit my performance. I seem to lack the 'killer instinct' that some people possess to take risks and push their mind and body right to its limit, although I suppose I would in a life-threatening situation. Even on occasions when I do 'complete' a particular challenge, I am sometimes left asking myself, "Yes you did it, but did you really do it in style?"

Does this mean that with many of the challenges I take on, I am doomed to feel afterwards that I have failed? The conundrum for me is how to reconcile my cautious risk-averse nature with my desire to have lots of enjoyable adventures:

- Adventures involve risk because they force you to push your normal boundaries and move you out of your comfort zone. They also expose you to the risk of failing.
- As a cautious person, I limit risk and avoid surprises wherever I can.
- So, how can I have adventures that I find enjoyable if I allow myself to feel I have 'failed' in many of the challenges I set myself?

Clearly, something has to give, and in my case I square the circle by the selective way that I apply the concept of 'success' to the challenges I attempt. I always experience a mixture of apprehension and excitement when I try to do something that I'm not sure I can do, and in many of the challenges I tackle I don't achieve all of the things that I set out to achieve. However even in those cases, as long as I enjoyed the overall experience, I rate the adventure that the challenge brought with it a 'success', and have a profound sense of having 'almost achieved'.

In my mind, I am quite content to feel that I have 'almost achieved' a challenge. I feel a warm positive glow, rather like when I have a shot of brandy in my coffee. I pat myself on the back and tell myself that if it's stretched me and moved me out of my comfort zone, and I have coped, then I have definitely achieved something. I know purists will say that 'almost achieved' is not grammatically correct, in the same way you can't say somebody is 'a bit pregnant', but it's the best I can do to convey my feelings.

It never feels like failure to me because my mindset is: "If it's been an adventure it's been a success". The 'journey' is more important to me than the objectives, and the adventure is reward enough. Afterwards my reaction is invariably, "I really enjoyed that, I guess I'll just have another go and try to do a better job next time."

For example, if I was climbing a mountain with the aim of planting a flag at the top, and with great effort after a difficult scramble, I managed to plant it somewhere near the top, my reaction as I descended would be, "What a great adventure this has been, and I almost achieved my aim of reaching the top."

I know that some may scoff and say this is a cop-out, but adopting this perspective has enabled me to have many adventures which have greatly added to my enjoyment of life, despite being a cautious person with only average abilities. We each have our own idea about what is adventurous. For some people my adventures will just be 'a walk in the park', while for others they will be 'doing the impossible'.

People who are competitive would be far harder on themselves than I am. You are likely to hear them say things such as, "Failure is not an option!" or "Let's just do it!" or "What have I got to lose?" Where I see success and 'almost achieving', they would see failure and would be disappointed and downcast.

Remember, I am only talking here about my attitude to the personal challenges that I undertake. I would hate to be told by my dentist or doctor that they really enjoyed their time at medical school, and had almost achieved a pass in their final exams!

One thing continues to baffle me though. On many of the challenges I tackle I am walking on my own in remote places, which is something I really enjoy doing, yet I acknowledge that walking alone involves significant risks. With my cautious nature, how do I reconcile taking such risks? The only explanation I can offer is that subconsciously, the cautious controlling side of me must calculate that by walking alone, the complete control I retain over where I go, how fast I go, when I stop, what I think about and what I do, trumps the risks that are involved. I guess in this case, I accept the risks as the price of freedom.

Wow, what an adventure!
(and I almost reached the top)

My family and friends not only ask me why I do the Ridgeway Challenge, but after completing it twice, can't understand why I want to attempt it yet again. I am a great believer in the idea that the reason people do things is that they are trying to fulfil a personal 'need'. However, having thought long and hard about it, I am no nearer understanding the 'need' that is motivating me to have another go.

To finish on a poetic note: all I know is that the Ridgeway Challenge forces me to draw on my inner reserves, which makes me feel truly alive. It feeds my soul, and that's a good enough reason for me.

My epitaph should be:

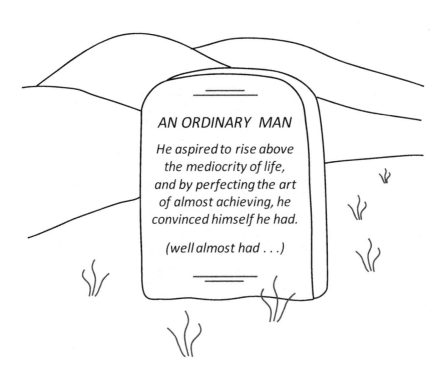

AN ORDINARY MAN

He aspired to rise above the mediocrity of life, and by perfecting the art of almost achieving, he convinced himself he had.

(well almost had . . .)

Other books by the author:

ROCKETS ORBITS AND NEWTON

Modelling a Rocket's flight to orbit in a spreadsheet

THE SOFT LANDING CHALLENGE

Modelling a Rocket's soft landing from orbit in a spreadsheet

LIGHT NEEDS TIME

Making sense of Einstein's Special Theory of Relativity

EINSTEIN AND THE DOVES OF DEIMOS

How the Doves affect space and time

More information is available on the author's website:

www.rocketsandrelativity.co.uk

Printed in Great Britain
by Amazon